ACCELERATE FINANCIALLY

ACCELERATE YOUR FINANCIAL GOALS AND WIN!

ACCELERATE FINANCIALLY

ACCELERATE YOUR FINANCIAL GOALS AND WIN!

BARRY L. MITCHELL, SR

Accelerate Financially

Accelerate Your Financial Goals and Win!

By,

Barry L. Mitchell, Sr.

Mitchell Enterprises Global Inc. (MEGI)

www.megiglobalinc.com

Editing, Cover and Interior Design: SheEO Publishing Company
www.SheEOPublishing.com

First Printing 2017

ISBN #: 978-0692867198

Disclaimer: The strategies provided in this book are financial recommendations and are not designed to substitute good judgment applicable to individual circumstances. The samples and examples are hypothetical and should not be taken as literal.

Published in the United States

TABLE OF CONTENTS

ABOUT THE AUTHOR

Barry L. Mitchell, Sr., served more than 25 years in the United States Navy and the United States Army at home and abroad. He retired in 2005 as a Lieutenant Colonel from the United States Army. He has served as an adjunct professor of management at institutions of higher learning on the East coast.

He is a certified public accountant (CPA) at his firm, Mitchell Certified Public Accountant (CPA) LLC, located in Woodbridge, Virginia. His practice specializes in both individual and business tax preparation and financial consulting. In addition, Barry is the Chief, Financial Officer for Wendy Mitchell Ministries, Inc., a 501c3 non-profit organization.

He is the Chief Executive Officer (CEO) of Mitchell Enterprises Global Inc. (MEGI), a government consulting firm. In this capacity, MEGI performed financial consulting work for the Department of the Army and Department of the Navy for more than eleven years. MEGI currently provides support to the United States Postal Service (USPS).

Barry is a real estate investor and currently owns, along with his wife, Wendy M. Mitchell, real estate holdings in multiple states. He resides in Triangle, Virginia, with his wife, Wendy M. Mitchell.

PREFACE

Think back to when you were in primary school; the smartest kid in class could not make you smart. You could not become knowledgeable by just wishing for it. You had to apply yourself to become intelligent. Well, achieving your personal goals in finance is no different. No one else can do for you what you can do for yourself.

Change is good only when it is applied. Everything starts with being open to accepting advice on how to go from where you are to where you want to be in your pursuit of wealth and financial independence.

This book is designed to motivate you to start thinking about your future. I share a range of topics for you to implement and make work for you. Some of the concepts I present, you may have heard before but may not have applied them to your life and dreams. Well, now is the time to apply these tried and true principles and move forward. My primary goal is to share a few simple suggestions that will accelerate our financial lives together as we review the concepts.

I encourage you to read the book for its guidance, take it seriously, acknowledge where you are, and do something different to change the financial path you are currently pursuing. I challenge every reader to passionately pursue his or her financial goals. Change the way you currently view your money and your future.

Make the change as if your financial life depends on it—because it does.

DEDICATION

To my dad, the late Jimmie Lee Mitchell, a man who loved his family and was full of wisdom. You could call on him anytime of the day or night. He always had time for you. I love and miss you, dad.

ACKNOWLEDGEMENTS

First, I want to thank God for my wife who inspired me to write this book. Thank you, Wendy, for always being there for me through the thick and the thin. I could not have sat down and begun to put pen to paper without your love, encouragement, prayers, and belief in me.

Thanks, Mom (Fannie Mitchell), for always instilling in me that with God all things are possible, and for your consistent level of love and caring displayed to me from the cradle until now. Thanks, Mom, for everything.

My children, Barry Jr. (BJ) and Benicia (Peaches), have always pushed me as a dad. They challenged me to be the best I could be without even knowing it. Thank you both.

I also want to thank my sisters, cousins, aunts, uncles, and grandparents who helped shape me into the person I am today.

I have met so many people in my life who have influenced me greatly. Many of them served in the military and became role models for me. I want to thank Guy Bennett (a retired Green Beret), the late Captain L. Wayne Rushing (retired Navy chaplain), the late Colonel Thaddeus Chapman (retired Army infantry), the late Lieutenant Colonel Charles Hobbs, Sr. (retired Army military police), the late Colonel J. Benjamin Hall (Army medical doctor) , the late 1st Class Petty Officer Theodore (Ted), Jr. and the late Mrs. Mattye Robinson, and Colonel Adam McKee, Jr. (retired Air Force veterinarian and Navy civil servant) for their military service and for playing a role in shaping my life.

I want to thank those individuals who aren't listed by name who helped me along my journey in life. Whether they were a school teacher, a principal, a neighbor, a military instructor, a college instructor, a pastor or a friend, their kindness and willingness to lend a hand did not go unnoticed.

Ultimately, I want to thank my Lord and Savior Jesus Christ for opening so many doors that were once closed to me. I share this with others not knowing what they believe in or who they believe in. (But for me and my house, we will serve the Lord.) I believe having a relationship with God is the initial and critical step towards success because it lays the foundation for all the other actions. I believe it is essential for your life if you want to soar in all areas. I urge you to accept Jesus Christ as your personal savior. Taking this bold step will not prevent bad things from happening, but it will give peace despite whatever may happen. God will grant us the serenity to accept the unpleasant things in this life and go on anyhow—not to mention you have a personal savior you can confide in any time of the day or night. It could be three o'clock in the morning on any given day, and God is right there to hear your petitions, desires, and anything else you wish to share with Him. He is never too busy or too far away.

Asking God to come into your life is to ask for a metamorphosis. My Bible tells me that God makes the difference in every situation, not just religious events. He also makes the difference in our health, wealth, emotions, relationships, jobs, careers, avocations, self-esteem, confidence—the list goes on. God is very much present in everything we do and say.

However, we must be bold enough to take the first step in pursuing a relationship with Him. I challenge you to review some of the Old Testament heroes—Abraham, Isaac, Jacob, Moses, Joseph, Daniel, and the three Hebrew boys (Shadrach, Meshach, and Abednego)—and see what God did for them. Yes, He did the unthinkable.

Let me bring this point closer to home and apply it to a modern-day child who God scooped out of sin and set his feet on solid ground. I'm talking about me. One thing all of us can attest to is what God has done for us.

INTRODUCTION

Most financial talk shows are intended for sophisticated investors who know what their goals are and have already put a plan into place to fulfill their vision. Such shows are great for people who understand Wall Street and can read stocks in financial publications. However, many people do not understand the complexities of finance. They do not know how to translate it in its simplest form.

Accelerate Financially presents the simplicity of finance. It is designed to assist the average person in taking control of his or her finances so they may flourish toward their personal financial goal. It is intended for those who do not know where or when to start and are not informed about how to read daily stocks trades.

Throughout this book, 10 recommendations are provided which are considered necessary to help financially shape the rest of your life:

1. To Thine Own Self Be True
2. Chart a course for your life
3. Put yourself in a position to get paid
4. Live debt-free
5. Make your money work for you
6. Establish and maintain positive relationships
7. Don't take no for an answer
8. *Carpe diem*
9. Self-actualize
10. Reach back and help others

The first few chapters focus on mindset. The remaining chapters focus on execution. At the end of each chapter, questions are presented that are designed for the reader to answer. Readers are encouraged to play fair; they are encouraged to not go to the next chapter until they are brutally honest with themselves about where they are today.

Financial success is not just for the smart or attractive; it is not for those who do more talking than performing. It is for anyone who wants it. It's for those who demonstrate more action than talk. It is ours for the asking.

Financial success is achievable but we must possess the intestinal fortitude to stay in the fight when our financial situations get tough. We must possess the love, the vision, and determination to nurture it and we must put in the effort, the time and the sacrifice to achieve it.

So if you're ready, let's begin to Accelerate!

CHAPTER 1

TO THINE OWN SELF BE TRUE

Let me begin chapter 1 with a testimony and share with you some of the adverse things that happened to me and how God brought me out with flying colors. What follows is my story.

I grew up in a small city about one hundred miles north of Miami, Florida. I was born into poverty. My parents, grandparents, uncles, and aunts were mostly migrants and poor. They were uneducated, and it showed on many fronts. Their lack of financial prowess led to many unfortunate circumstances. For example, I remember my parents often had to decide whether to pay the rent or the electric bill in certain months because there wasn't enough money to pay both.

As migrants they had to rely on the weather and the growth of the citrus and vegetable crops for their livelihood. If it rained, it was a lost day because they were unable to go to work and earn any money. That's how my life was shaped. That was the lifestyle I knew. No other vision was available to me at that time. The citrus work in Florida was seasonal as were other crops. But the bills did not stop when the seasons changed. So when school was over, my parents and other relatives would pack up and head north to find work in other states during the summer.

Even though I lived and traveled as a migrant along with my parents and other family members, yet God allowed me thus far to fulfill my destiny. How? By becoming an author, an entrepreneur, a professor, a CPA, a father, a grandfather, a military officer, a deacon and the list goes on. I share this with you to encourage you to admit where you are and what you have gone through. Then make up in your mind to go for it all. After all, what do you really have to lose? Nothing.

Unless you are among the select few people whose rich relatives will leave you a fortune, most of us have to gain financial security the old-fashioned way—by earning it!

However, we must ask ourselves, are we ready for change? Are we ready to give up some pleasure to achieve some level of success? Are we ready for the challenge?

We may aspire to excel or achieve something great but if we are not willing to make the necessary sacrifices to reach the goals or life-long ambitions, we will not reach them. If we are not willing to put in the work, we will not excel. If we are not actually working, we will not actually produce.

As stated in William Shakespeare's *Hamlet*, it is the romantics' famed proverb, "To thine own self be true," we must admit where we are right now. If you are in debt, then admit that you are in debt. Conversely, if you have $1 million saved, then officially admit that you are a millionaire. Do not pretend or placate the situation. Be transparent at the beginning of your journey regarding what you might not have accomplished when you were young and vibrant. Understand that life is not over even if you missed some critical windows, such as graduating from college at age 22, securing your first professional job at 23, buying your first home at 30, and getting married and starting a family at 31. Or maybe you're divorced, have fathered or given birth to a child out of wedlock, have served time in prison, or lost someone special you miss dearly. Whatever has happened in our lives has happened. It's a new day—and it is not too late to start fresh. We have a chance every day to start over and redo what we should have done the previous day. There's still time. So if you are ready to start from where you are now, let's get on the road to success.

Acceleration Tip #1: Write a Financial Plan

For you to move forward in your finances, it is imperative to know where your money goes. Every individual should have a written financial plan. Some call it a budget. Others call it a roadmap to where you're going in the short- and long-term. A financial plan records what comes in and what goes out each day, week, month, quarter, and, ultimately, year. The plan becomes your guide to where you want to be in a year, five years, 10 years, and someday retirement. It has been said that if an individual invests $100 per month earning

8% return annually starting at age 21 and continuing this strategy until age 65, they could amass almost half a million dollars.

I believe advancement in technology is useful, but accelerating your finances requires you to get involved personally.

First, list all your monthly income—salary, pension, investments, alimony—then list all your expenses including rent or mortgage, car payment and maintenance, credit cards, loans, groceries, utilities, insurance, cable, phone, entertainment, clothes, child support, charity, etc.

Make this list of expenses as extensive as possible so that you can see where all your money is going.

Example:

Income	**Amount**		**Expenses**	**Amount**
Salary			Rent/Mortgage	
Pension			Car Payment	
Investment			Credit Cards	
Alimony			Groceries	

Then compare what's coming in against what's going out and see if you can make some adjustments. You need to go through each expense to see what is necessary and what an indulgence is. For now, you may need to curtail habits like eating out at restaurants and impulse buying.

This process requires clear-eyed self-examination to see how serious you are about gaining control of your financial future. You are center stage, and you must make the call. This essential step must be conquered before you can begin to grow your net worth. You must arrest your spending habits and do it quickly.

Many people do not have a budget. That is probably truer now than ever because many routine tasks are done by computers or some form of technology.

Once this step is achieved, you can begin to shape the rest of your financial life.

Chapter Questions – To Thine Own Self Be True

Are you in debt (credit cards, school loans, mortgage, car loans, consumer credit, etc.) up to your eyeballs?

If the answer is yes, *stop spending now*. Cease using any more credit cards or requesting additional financing. Write out a budget. Make it a point to ensure that the money you have coming in does not exceed what you have going out. Of the all the questions asked in this summary, this is probably the most important. To move forward, you must exert self-control over your finances and not spend more than what you bring in.

- ***Have you done all the right things but still can't seem to get ahead financially and grow your net worth?*** If your answer is yes, then create a financial plan tailored to your specific situation and goals and follow it. Then review all 10 must-do steps in this book and apply them to every area of your life.
- ***Are you ready to take control of your financial life and excel?*** If the answer is yes, take the actions addressed in each chapter and apply them. Do not give up the first time a strategy doesn't work or if something you tried didn't result in a positive outcome. Try again. Persistence always gets results. Quitting never gets results.
- ***Did you finish high school?*** If the answer is no, search for local adult education or general education development (GED) programs in your area. You can do an online search or visit a resource center in a library to begin your quest to attain your high school education. Some of these programs are fully funded by a non-profit agency or local government.
- ***Do you feel you have you parented a child too soon?*** If the answer is yes, forgive yourself and move on. Whatever you forfeited during this time, you can pursue now or in the future.
- ***Did you attend college or trade school when you had the opportunity?*** If the answer is no, contact schools in your area to see how you can enroll. Do not forget to research whether you qualify for any grants or other financial assistance.
- ***Have you served time in prison?*** If the answer is yes, forgive yourself and remain clean and honest going forward in your life. You can still pursue your passion despite your criminal record. You can achieve the highest goals you have set for yourself. You could own a business, become a doctor, become a minister, or whatever aspiration you may have.

It depends on the actions you take today and those in the future. It is up to you.

- ***Do you feel sorry for yourself?*** If the answer is yes, stop it. Step up and begin to reshape your life. Start making good decisions that will benefit you and those you love. Take baby steps in the direction you need to go. For example, if you are out of work, start applying for jobs. If you don't have the skills to seek employment, then enroll in a technical college or a program that allows you to learn the necessary skills to attain a good paying job. You are responsible for you. No other person is responsible for you. Ask for help when needed.

CHAPTER 2

CHART A COURSE FOR YOUR LIFE

It is incumbent upon each of us to identify our passion and our purpose. We should examine what ignites our desire to move forward. We have to make up our mind to strive to achieve something great. We must establish goals for our lives. These goals should represent who we are and what we want to do in life. If our goal is to become the president of the United States, then we should get into local politics. If it is to become an astronaut, then we should find out what the criteria are and get the necessary education and experience to become an astronaut. Do not simply wish for change. Set a plan.

Goals are important because they drive our behavior into accomplishing the unthinkable. No one wakes up one morning, decides they are going to be a doctor, and gets accepted to the college of their choice that afternoon. Achieving goals requires careful planning and coordination from beginning to end. If we are not engaged in this endeavor, we may end up in a financial scenario we do not prefer.

If we dream big, then big things will happen to us. Conversely, if we dream small, then small things will happen to us. If we never dream, we will never get anywhere.

Acceleration Tip #2 – Map out your financial goals

Charting a course for your life is like going on a journey; you need to plan a specific route on how to get from where you are now to where you think you want to go. The course selected requires careful planning and a deliberate choice in what path to choose. The best way to accomplish this step is to put your ideas in writing. Success is defined in different ways by different people. For some it is defined as having a million dollars; for others it is defined as being healthy, happy, of sound mind, having good family relationships, or enjoying steady employment. Write out your overall goals and define what success is to you.

Example:

My overall financial goals are:
Financial Success to me is:
Within one year I would like to have accomplished_____ financially:
In five years I would like to have:
In ten years, I desire to:

Nearly all of our plans for the future require money. We must take charge of our financial journey. Exhibiting the appropriate behavior, such as determination and drive, is a must for charting the course for our lives. When we embark upon a career path and genuinely mean to accomplish it, the desire takes residence in our very fiber. It consumes us, and we will not stop until we have reached our goal.

Conversely, if we do not chart this course, we will bounce from pillar to post, becoming fiscally unproductive. If we do not expend our time and money wisely, we may find ourselves 10 or 15 years behind where we should be. If we do not make the critical decisions and the necessary actions when we are supposed to, time will not wait on us. It keeps on ticking. And before we know it, life will pass us by.

The world in which we live permits us the opportunity to choose our path in life. Our financial beginnings do not matter. Once we begin the economic journey, we should not allow anyone to deter us or stop us. A doable and clear financial plan can help us remain focused and be successful when opposition comes.

Chart a Course for Your Life–Chapter Questions

Does the job you are currently performing line up with what you had in mind for your life?

Are you willing to put in the time and effort needed to have financial security? A job gets you by; a career secures your future.

Have you charted a course for your life? If the answer is no, then start today and begin to chart a course for where you want to go in life. It doesn't matter where you are currently. You have to start from somewhere. And you might as well as start now.

- ***What is it that you want to do with the rest of your life?*** Choose a career. Then write down a list of what it will take to achieve it. It may require going back to college or maybe even finishing high school first, which can be done by getting a general education degree (GED) or attending night school. Whatever is required, do it!
- ***Did you put some thought into what you want to be/do?*** If the answer is no, please do some introspection, then change your direction if your inner self is telling you to do so. Make your choice feel good.
- ***Did you seek out others while charting your course?*** If the answer is no, that's okay. However, if you're not sure about the process, then ask for help. There are many free resources available listed online and in your local library resource center.
- ***Did you get turned away or discouraged in charting your course?*** If the answer is yes, don't let anyone influence you not to move forward in life. Do it because it is what you want to do.

CHAPTER 3

PUT YOURSELF IN A POSITION TO GET PAID

Some inventors have become wealthy by creating innovative and forward-thinking items that have revolutionized the world. Others have found success with the simplest inventions. Nonetheless, one common step each of these inventors took was to share their goods or services with the world. They did not just settle for being an inventor or entrepreneur. They followed through and brought the product to market.

We possess that same level of talent and potential that the individuals who founded multinational corporations possess. We are capable of achieving the same level of greatness that major power brokers—past and present— have achieved.

It has been said that the cemetery is filled with great ideas and fantastic stories. Meaning too many people never took the opportunity to live out their dreams and become all they should have become. They took their ideas, skills, and talents with them to the grave, meaning they died never fulfilling them. We do not want to do that. We want to give it all we have and leave nothing for the grave. We do not want anybody to say you did not give your all—or exercise your gifts or talents fully.

There are so many ideas, creations, and strategies waiting for us to discover. People will pay for our knowledge or our talent. The most important thing is choosing something we have a passion for or at least enjoy doing. We should select a profession or career that we enjoy doing so much that we would do it for free. Our enthusiasm and dedication and competency will make others happy to pay us—usually handsomely.

Acceleration Tip #3 – Don't Be Afraid to Step Out

Know your worth and do not be afraid to ask for it. Step out. Do not sell yourself short. Get paid what you deserve, regardless if you are in a white-collar profession like banking or a skilled trade such as an electrician. Recognize that you have too much talent and smarts not to be paid well. No matter where you are in your professional life today, it is never too late to change course, go in the direction you desire, and get paid when you get there.

Chapter Questions

- ***Do you have a skill that puts you in a position to be highly compensated***? If the answer is no, you must decide whether you desire to change what you are doing. If you answer yes, then you should determine how to get paid what you are worth.
- ***Are you good with your hands or your head?*** This question is designed to assist you in honing your skilled craft. If you are extremely proficient with your hands, you should attend a technical school that will equip you with skills necessary to become certified in your chosen endeavor. Conversely, if you are quick with your head and you prefer an office environment and analytical work, then you may want to pursue college or advanced collegiate studies.
- ***Do you have the resources to attend a technical college or a traditional college, if applicable?*** If the answer is no, then research the various programs available in your local town, city, state, or even the federal government. There is a myriad of programs available to assist you in attending a school of higher learning, such as a federal Pell grant. States have similar programs. Nonprofits aid with attending college and technical schools. The Veterans Administration (VA) offers tremendous educational programs for those who have served honorably.
- ***Are you motivated to start something new because you want to be paid what you are worth?*** If the answer is yes, it is yours for the asking. This means there are both organizations and opportunities that are waiting for you.

There are jobs that go unfilled because there aren't enough qualified professionals to fill them. Examples include becoming equipment operators, cyber security, IT, machine operators, large construction equipment operators, and using highly complex equipment. However, once you receive the appropriate training to match the list of jobs that go unfilled, you will have transitioned to a position where the world should pay you what you are worth.

- ***Are you ready to begin this new journey of changing your position for the better?*** If the answer is yes, follow the guidance so far. Identify what you want to do, research what skills you possess, assess what you want to do with the rest of your life, research what local programs are available, review all the programs that are on the Internet and in your local area that can help you get started, and take action. If necessary, take baby steps toward the charted course you are currently on.

CHAPTER 4

LIVE DEBT-FREE

To me, this is the most exciting chapter of this book because we begin our financial life. It is where we draw a line in the sand and engage in financial development.

I was once also caught in the mindset of having to finance almost everything I wanted, until I realized one day that there was a better way to purchase assets (homes, cars, jewelry, clothes, etc.) than on credit.

Debt is not always bad, but there is a better alternative; it's called living debt-free. It is the new American dream. If we can outsmart debt, we will be the better for it. To live debt-free is to have complete freedom over how and when you decide to spend your hard-earned money.

The world thrives on people financing almost every item they believe is a must-have, from cars to homes, cell phones to a steady stream of gadgets. The ease with which we can pay on time gets us in trouble.

Do you know how many financial lives have been ruined by debt? Most individuals who have a mortgage are one or two paychecks away from losing their home. You can buy a home with a 30-year mortgage and pay faithfully for 20 years. But one day, you may lose your job and become unable to pay the mortgage. The bank or mortgage company who gave you the mortgage will have a local deputy sheriff evict you from your house. Sometimes individuals have to be shocked into choosing an alternative to debt.

Debt even has adverse consequences on a country. Consider the United States' (US) national debt, which is $19.4 trillion as of this writing. The US must borrow money to meet its daily financial obligations. Interest accrues daily. It is out of control.

Federal and personal debt are like identical twins. They both gnaw at us until something unpleasant happens. Do you realize that when we buy a car or house, we pay a daily interest rate for using the bank's or mortgage company's money? Say someone borrows $77,500 at a 3.24% annual interest rate on an interest-only loan. The borrower is assessed $6.95 interest per day for the use of the money. Since it is interest only, the loan payment would go on forever because nothing is paid towards reducing the $77,500 principal. That means you would pay $6.95/day forever unless you start to pay something on the principal. Most of these loans permit interest-only payments for the first 10 years, making them appealing to buyers who plan to sell their home within that period since they won't have to pay principal toward the loan.

Another example is when you purchase items with credit cards, they end up costing you double, triple, quadruple, and sometimes as high as five times over the original price. I am not anti-credit; however, I want you to know what you are signing up for when you buy on credit. Yes, it is a convenience to get something now rather than saving up and paying for it in cash. Although credit is great to have, it can put you in bondage without you realizing that you are accumulating massive amounts of debt. I want you to know that you have options and you don't have to pay more than the original price for items.

If a home cost $400,000 and you finance it at 3% for 30 years, the actual cost of the loan would be $607,110, or $207,110 in interest. While this is not necessarily a tragedy, do you want to pay more than you have to?

The answer is generally no for most of us, so we need to minimize credit. First, you have to change the way you think about money by comparing how you spend money with your short- and long-term goals in mind. You have to know what you want out of life. Say you decide you want to retire by age 55. If you are currently 35 years old, that's only 20 years to go from where you are today to where you want to be. You will have to do some backward planning and take serious steps to retire in 20 years. Some of the questions that need to be asked include:

- Will your home be paid off or will you have a mortgage?
- Will you have any credit card debt?
- Will you have saved enough for your retirement?
- Do you even have some form of retirement?

- Will you have a car note?
- Will you have any consumer debt that is serviced monthly?
- Will you have a child or children in college?
- Will you receive a pension?
- Do you have affordable medical insurance?
- Do you have adequate life insurance?
- Will you have long-term care insurance?
- Does anyone rely on you for financial support (aging parent, child, or sibling)?

Also keep in mind that as of this writing, the minimum age to receive Social Security, without being disabled, is 62; to qualify for Medicare is 65, if not linked to disability.

The point I am making here is that retiring early requires a whole new set of rules. You have to plan. A major shift has to occur in your thinking about money, in how and where you spend your money, and in learning how to delay spending until you have sufficient funds to purchase whatever it is that you want. If these new behaviors are not learned, you will not achieve your goal of retiring at age 55.

Adopting a debt-free mindset is a 180-degree turn from what society teaches us — to live life now. It also teaches us to build and maintain an excellent credit score. Having a high credit rating is okay, but it can put in you the mindset of wanting to borrow to purchase a home, a car, and other major items on credit, thereby paying significantly more when paid off over time. Society also emphasizes the importance of buying the expensive car, the big house in the suburbs, the jewelry, and going on lavish vacations, but you're not encouraged to wait until you have earned or saved enough money to buy these things.

I am not saying you cannot have these items, because you can. I encourage everyone to get whatever you desire. But ensure this one principle is present: make sure you can pay for it. Living with a debt-free mindset will accelerate you financially fourfold. Goals you set out to accomplish will occur sooner and without the added stress that comes with trying to save when your finances are maxed out. Being debt-free sets you apart from everyone else.

Imagine for a moment that all your major liabilities — car note, mortgage, credit card debt, student loan, etc. —were paid off. Think of what you could accomplish with your finances. You could give more to charity. Or give more to family or friends. You could purchase — in cash — the sports car you always wanted. Being debt-free is a phenomenon. It has properties and a life of its own. Also it will set you apart from others because you are no longer in bondage to your house, your car, or to debt. You have been set free.

Acceleration Tip #4–How do you become debt-free?

Below are my recommendations:

- Change the way you think about money and how best to use it for your benefit.
- Establish a budget early on in your working life. Most people don't like budgets, but they are worth their weight in gold. Establishing a budget is just like following a compass, which directs one whether to go straight, turn right, or turn left. It tells you where you are going and how you are going to get there.
- When possible, plan your purchases by setting aside money each time you get paid. Let's say your washer or dryer needs to be replaced. The cost is $500 to replace both. In your budget, you are going to allocate your paycheck for all your monthly expenses. This includes saving to buy a new washer and dryer. While you are saving, you may have to go to the laundromat to wash clothes. That's what I was referring to when I said you have to change the way you think. Making a change isn't easy. But change is required if you want to become debt-free. For example, when you allocate money for a specific purpose, here is what the process looks like :

  Income: $2500
  Expenses:
  Rent $750
  Tithe $250
  Food $150
  Car note $250
  Credit Card Payment $50
  Gas for the Car $75
  Electric Bill $100
  Gas Bill for House $50

Cell Phone $75
Water and Sewer $50
Entertainment $75
Emergency $100
Eating Out $65
Savings $150
Car Maintenance $50
Appliance Maintenance $50
Home Security $38
Hair care $100
Other expenses $72

This financial sample helps identify every dollar earned and steers it in the direction that it needs to go—including emergencies.

- Try as much as possible to use the previous three steps to buy everything in cash, including your house, car, vacations, and eating out. This sounds simple, but it is very difficult to do because the desire to have something now rather than later generally wins over waiting. No one wants to wait and plan. Everyone wants their toys now! The now syndrome is what gets us into deep, deep trouble with debt. The luxury car and home bought on credit now cause us to derail far bigger financial victories that are waiting for us. We simply can't say no to easy credit, easy finance, or the low-interest loan. That is why it takes a commitment to wait, save, and then pay cash for whatever it is you want.
- Dream a little. Imagine what you could do with your time and your money if you were debt-free. Some people desire to devote more time to charity or helping others. However, they do not have the luxury of not working and must remain in the rat race. This new debt-free perspective gives you a refreshing view on how your life can be. But you must buy into it and let it take you where you want to go.

  Going from being a debt connoisseur to being debt-free will change your life in ways you cannot even comprehend. Here's what I mean. If you are debt-free, you could:
- Buy a new car, home, clothes, fund your children or grandchildren's college education, go on vacation,

donate more to your church, give more to charity, help family or friends financially, and live on your terms as it relates to finances.

- Choose to work or not
- Choose to buy or not.
- Choose to help or not, financially.
- Choose to volunteer.
- Get your time back. Time is now yours to plan the day, the week, the month, or the year (with God's input of course) how you desire.

Chapter Questions

- ***Have you changed the way you think about your money and how you spend your money?*** If you checked no, before you can speak the words *debt-free*, you have to change the way you think about money and how you spend your money. Whether you said yes or no, it's imperative that this step is mastered first. Your thinking is linked directly to your successful accomplishment of becoming debt-free.
- ***Have you identified what your financial goals are?*** If the answer is no, this is a very important step in moving in the direction of being debt-free. You have to highlight or know where it is you want to go or what you want to accomplish because all the remaining decision-making rests on what direction you are heading. Identify those goals now. A goal might be to pay off credit card debt. If that's the case, stop spending. Then call your credit card company and ask them if they would lower your credit card interest rate or reduce your monthly payment. Ask if they would waive or reduce the amount you owe because you are going through a financial reinvention. Try anything legal that will help reduce your credit card debt. This is just an example. Other financial goals might be to pay a home off sooner or pay a car off sooner. All these examples will point you in the direction that you want to go.
- ***Do you have a budget that you follow?*** If the answer is no, as I stated previously, a budget is worth its weight in gold. It literally puts you on the path to success. A budget, however, must be taken seriously and followed. If you are not interested in accomplishing your goal, then do not create

a budget. But if you are committed to achieving your goals, then begin your financial comeback.

- ***Have you taken action to become debt-free?*** If the answer is no, then implement the steps above and begin this journey. Start right where you are.

CHAPTER 5

MAKE YOUR MONEY WORK FOR YOU

We all work hard for our money. But it is important that your money works hard for you. Have you ever wondered why the rich get richer and why the middle class keeps on working and doesn't get richer? Have you ever wondered why some make their money grow and others don't? Well, one of the key reasons is that most of us fail to educate ourselves about how to grow wealth. This chapter talks about getting educated about your money.

The rich take advantage of America's financial engines. One of the strategies the rich use is to invest in the stock market. I am not advising anyone to invest in the stock market. I am simply sharing with you one of the ways the rich get richer. They invest in companies by purchasing their stock. The rich buy stocks when they are low and sell them when they are high, thereby generating huge amounts of wealth.

However, you can also lose money in the stock market. When it comes to growing your money, there is always going to be a risk. You have to decide whether you are going to stay with the tried and true, such as a regular savings account, or attempt to increase your wealth while minimizing your risk as much as possible. No one wants to lose their hard-earned money. But you need to become informed about what is available to help grow your nest egg. Then you need to act on that information with wisdom, vision, and confidence in your financial goal. There is nothing wrong with a regular savings account. But outperforming inflation over time will probably not happen.

The second financial engine the rich use is creating businesses. There are tons of businesses in the marketplace. They have grown from momandpop shops to behemoths. Some have mushroomed into multinational corporations.

Another financial engine the rich take advantage of is real estate. As you homeowners know, the house most of you purchased five years ago has increased in value since that time. I say most because some may be underwater — where the home is worth less than what the homeowner owes on it. But in general, homes increase in value. Rich real estate owners use the same principal as stock investors: they buy low and sell high. Most of the wealthy accepted the risk when they purchased these properties that have since increased in value.

A financial engine that most employees use is investing in the retirement programs at work. The self-employed can establish individual retirement accounts (IRAs) formally called simplified employee pension (SEP) IRAs by the Internal Revenue Service (IRS). When it comes to investing, you generally need time to grow your money. It is not grown overnight, so financial experts recommend you start saving for retirement as soon as possible. No age is too young to start saving because we all know that every financial segment — stocks, real estate, gold, silver, oil, and commodities — will fluctuate. But over time, all these segments show tremendous growth.

Just as the rich and super rich take advantage of every known financial engine to increase their wealth, I encourage you consider some of these vehicles as your rocket propels you forward financially.

Acceleration Tip#5 — Specific Ways to Grow Your Wealth

- Reprogram your mind about how to make your money grow.
- Use compound interest to help grow your fortune. Compound interest will cause your money to double, triple, and quadruple if you invest in the right vehicle at the right time. Compound interest is when you invest a principal balance and that principal balance accrues interest for a period of time (i.e., a year). The second year includes the principal plus interest from the first year. Year three includes the principal plus interest from

years one and two. This method continues until your money actually increases in value and the evidence is clear about the multiplying effect of compounding interest.

Here's an example of the powerful effect of compounding interest. Your credit union/bank is paying 2.1% if you invest in a certificate of deposit for seven years. The return on your investment is $1,000 x 2.1% x 7 years.

Year	Balance	Rate	Total Interest
Year 1	$1,000.00	0.021	21
Year 2	$1,021.00	0.021	21.441
Year 3	$1,042.44	0.021	21.89126
Year 4	$1,064.33	0.021	22.35098
Year 5	$1,086.68	0.021	22.82035
Year 6	$1,109.50	0.021	23.29958
Year 7	$1,132.80	0.021	23.78887

Total interest over seven years: $156.59

From your initial, one-time investment of $1,000, you now have $1,156.59. Over seven years, you earned a total of $156.59. This example demonstrates that by saving $1,000 in a CD, you have employed compounding interest in your financial vision.

- Develop and apply your financial goals in charting a course for your life.
- Become educated about what investment vehicles are available and how they work.
- Determine what investments fit your financial profile. Do you want to invest in stocks, bonds, real estate, annuities, certificates of deposit, or money market funds?
- Determine your risk level. Can you afford to lose money if you invest in the stock market? Do you prefer investments that are 100% safe and backed by the Federal Deposit Insurance Corporation (FDIC) and/or the Federal Credit Union Association (FCUA), up to $250,000 per account/depositor?
- Review the pros and cons of investing in some type of IRA. The traditional and Roth IRA are good long-term investment strategies to implement in a portfolio aimed

at retirement. The IRA is a positive investment because the earnings are tax deferred, meaning non-taxable until withdrawn at retirement. The Roth is unique because you pay tax on the money going into this type of IRA so future withdrawals are tax free. However, there are eligibility requirements and may be contribution limitations, so you need to research to see if this type of investment works for you.

- Compare credit unions to banks when contemplating on where put to your money. Generally, credit unions pay higher interest rates on savings and certificates of deposit and charge lower rates on auto and home loans (if you must have a loan). Do your due diligence. Shop around at both banks and credit unions.
- Consider investing in a business. Do you have the personality to start a business? It takes a special person to start a business and make it successful. But a business can make you wealthy over time. Investing in a business requires some soul searching. There aren't sick days or holidays off unless you have employees working for you. When you have employees, you are then responsible for their payroll and paying payroll taxes to federal, state, and local governments. You must also market what it is you do. There is a lot involved in running a business. But most of the millionaires and billionaires on the *Forbes* wealthiest Americans list are business owners. This is just food for thought.
- Invest in your 401k/403b pension at your job/ employment. One of the surest and easiest ways to plan for retirement is to invest in your job's retirement program. Consider making the maximum 401ks/403bs contributions at your job, if possible. By not investing in your job's retirement plan, you are literally throwing money away. For every dollar you invest, your employer matches it. You invest $1, and the employer contributes a matching $1. You now have two, tax-deferred dollars in your retirement account. Tax deferred is important because it means you don't pay taxes until later when you are in a lower tax bracket and more than likely retired.

- Do tax planning. Pay your fair share of federal, state, and local taxes. However, don't pay any more than you are legally required to. This is something the average American does not do. Very few individuals project what their federal and state tax bills will be a year or two from now. You can lessen the impact of taxes by laying out a plan to manage the tax bill before it occurs.
- Use discounts and coupons. Not paying the regular price for consumer goods is a surefire way to save. There are discounts available to a variety of groups. For example, the military, seniors, students, and first responders are offered a discount at selected establishments. You can also find discounts online for a variety of purchases. You may need to ask for a discount because it won't necessarily be posted. Discounts are available on everything from groceries to auto repair to buying a house. Some people may feel ashamed and will not ask for it, but it doesn't hurt to ask.
- Consider purchasing rental properties. I am not referring to the infomercials on TV that cost you thousands of dollars and deliver next to nothing in terms of results. Strategically, do your due diligence and talk to a friend or neighbor who you trust that may be in the real estate profession and can help you. It's possible to grow a slow fortune in real estate over time if this is right for you.
- Research and master the dollar cost averaging concept. Dollar cost averaging allows an individual to invest in a mutual fund a fixed amount of money each month for many years. A mutual fund is an investment vehicle made up of funds collected from many investors that are invested in securities such as stocks, bonds, and money markets. Mutual funds are operated by money managers, who invest the fund's capital to produce capital gains and income for the fund's investors. One of the main advantages of mutual funds is they give small investors access to professionally managed, diversified financial portfolios.

  The amount invested could be $100 per month, which occurs monthly no matter what the economy does or doesn't do. Over very long periods of time, most mutual funds return 8 to 10% per year. Most individuals don't take advantage of this investing opportunity.

- Select an age you to desire to retire. If you are 30 years old and you want to retire by age 66, then that means you have 36 years to save and invest. Plan backward on how you are going to reach that goal. Choosing a retirement age sets your compass in the direction you want to go and tells you what you should be doing now at age 30 to reach the milestone you desire by age 66.
- Consolidate or negotiate loans when possible. If it's a mortgage, consider getting a 15-year or shorter loan. Give biweekly payments a look as an alternative to finance your home—half payments every two weeks. Since there are 52 weeks in a year, you'd make 26 half payments, or 13 full payments, which adds up to one extra full payment a year. This can shorten a standard 30-year loan by nearly five years.

  Another strategy is to split your mortgage and pay half on the 15th of the month and a half on the 30th. Over time this will reduce the amount of interest you are paying and therefore reduce the length of the mortgage, usually by a couple of months.

  The point here is neither method required new money, but both reduced the amount of interest that would accrue over the life of the loan.
- If you must have a credit card, use it to your fullest advantage. You should possess a credit card that offers cash back based on a point system. Once you accumulate a certain level/number of points, the credit card company will reward you with either cash, gift cards, or reimbursement for airline tickets.
- Get multiple estimates. When you are contemplating on making a major purchase (home, car, appliance, etc.), always get three estimates. I know this sounds routine. But you would be amazed at the difference in prices when you shop around. In the same purchase mode, apply discounts and other markdowns on this purchase. The amount you save could be as much as 10 to 15%. If an item is scratched or dented during shipment, you can ask for a discount. This simple but effective approach works every time. Remember, the goal is to make your

money work for you. And this includes paying less for an item.

Take action. After you have done all the previous steps required, you must act.

Multiple Income Sources

The next principle I want to share is that everyone should have multiple sources of income. This could include rental property income, long- and short-term investments (certificates of deposit, money market funds, dividends from individual stocks, and mutual fund appreciation, and annuity income) pensions, bonds, etc. When you have multiple income streams, you are not relying on one source of income. But the average individual has only one source of income. When this income is taken away, most are not able to adapt. Some even commit suicide.

The bible says, you want to be the lender and not the borrower. If your job lays you off, you will not be happy about this. But you also will not be destitute because you would have created and developed for yourself more income sources. You must create a stream of income sources.

Savings

You must have a mind to save on a recurring basis. Don't spend all your money and forget to allocate some for savings. Generally, saving on a monthly basis works better for most people. Then it depends on what you feel comfortable or safe putting your money into. Some people like savings accounts or CDs where their money is 100% safe up to $250,000, the amount insured by the FDIC or the FCUA. Others prefer to be on the precipice with stocks and new companies launching their initial public offering (IPO). It just depends on what you prefer.

But the point is you need to do something to cause your money to grow. Imagine your money is working for you while you are sleeping. Isn't that ideal? How about fantastic! Maybe you can only afford to invest in your 401k/403b at work. That is a great first start. Whatever you do, start somewhere in making your money work for you.

Chapter Questions

- ***Are you living paycheck to paycheck now?*** If the answer is yes, develop a plan to change that. You may have to change the type of work you do. It may require getting retrained in another career field to increase your earnings. Remember the principles discussed in Chapter III of putting yourself in a position to get paid.
- ***Are you aware of the financial vehicles available to you to make your money grow?*** If the answer is no, review your budget to compare your income with your expenses, looking to see if there is money remaining to invest. If there is, use it for a certificate of deposit, individual stocks, mutual funds, annuity, savings bonds, money market fund, rental property, etc., to help your money work for you. If you lack knowledge, seek out help from your banker or another financial professional you trust, who can share the basic principles of investing and what products the local bank/financial firm offers. The key is to acquire knowledge, so seek experts in their respective investment profession.
- ***Are you investing in your company's 401k/403b at work?*** If the answer is no, why not? You can't afford not to invest in it. By not investing, you are losing valuable time. Employees are on their own when it comes to planning for retirement. There are two types of retirement programs: defined benefit and defined contribution. Defined benefit—the dinosaur that is just about extinct—is where your company pays you a certain amount in retirement in exchange for your years of service and position at the time of retirement. This program is all but dead.

  Defined contribution—which has replaced defined benefit—is the 401k option of saving for retirement. The 403b is the governmental and nonprofit version. Funds invested in these programs are tax-deferred until you reach retirement and start to withdraw funds to live on. Defined contribution means you are on your own when it comes to planning for your retirement.
- ***Have you considered investing in individual stocks?*** If the answer is no, consider doing research on the history of the stock market. Two major events are going to stick out: 1929 and 2008. The first date was when the stock market crashed,

the start of the Great Depression. The other is the financial crisis/subprime mortgage debacle. This was characterized by financial institutions offering mortgages to anyone that was breathing, whether they qualified or not financially. It proved to be disastrous. However, history shows that over time the stock market grows by leaps and bounds and outperforms inflation. You need to understand the stock market and its volatility before deciding to participate in the market.

- ***Have you considered investing in mutual funds?*** If the answer is no, consider it. Mutual funds reduce the risk of investing in a single company. Over time a mutual fund will grow larger than inflation. One of your goals is to have your money outperform inflation so you can exist financially for years to come.
- ***Have you considered starting a business?*** If the answer is no, do your research to determine what a business entails. Equally important is to understand the work and sacrifice required as well as to know the rewards and wealth a business can generate for you. You must weigh the pros and cons when it comes to starting and running a business. Starting a business is a way to have your money work for you.
- ***Do you have multiple streams of income?*** If the answer is no, why not? You want to ensure that you have more than a paycheck or a pension coming in each month. Some of your options for generating multiple streams of income are a rental property, annuity, certificate of deposit, mutual funds, and individual stock.
- ***Do you know what your risk tolerance level is?*** If the answer is no, determine how much risk you are willing to take when it comes to investing. Do you feel more comfortable with investing in fixed investments, such as CDs, money market funds, and savings bonds that are backed by the federal government or the FDIC/FCUA? Or do you prefer to take risks in the stock market and mutual funds, with the expectation of great returns?
- ***Have you considered buying a rental property?*** If the answer is no, conduct some research on the pros and cons of owning rental real estate. It can be a headache. But it also can offer tremendous returns on your investment. Once

again, you have to weigh the risks versus the benefits to be derived.

CHAPTER 6

ESTABLISH AND MAINTAIN POSITIVE RELATIONSHIPS

One of the essential things about creating and growing wealth is having relationships with people from all walks of life. Some of these individuals are honest, and others are dishonest. Some of these professionals and lay people can share information that will help you achieve your financial goals. We need someone who we trust and can confide in regarding what it is that we want to do.

One of your goals may be to save $1 million by age 45. Who should you talk to about this aspiration? Who can you trust? What financial instruments should you invest in to accomplish this goal? Establishing and maintaining positive relationships is a major milestone in the quest to accelerate our financial lives forever. What you don't know can hurt you. And what you don't know, you can't do. And who you know can also hurt you. If an individual is unscrupulous, there is a possibility they will scam you out of every penny you have.

Many people have accumulated wealth and then lost it all because their money managers were either inept or dishonest. You need to find people who are going to help you reach your financial goals and not put you in a position where you can lose all your wealth. The person you connect with needs to have integrity, ethics, intelligence, expertise with investments, and honesty—someone you can count on.

Positive relationships beget other positive relationships. It takes one to know one. When you have positive relationships with a positive person, you can get to where you are trying to go quicker, safer, fairer, and honestly.

It can be hard to know who the right person is to trust with your money. An example is Bernie Madoff; he was highly respected, and yet he turned out to be a fraud and con artist. Many honest and hard-working people lost lots of money. The amount recovered was pennies on the dollar. So if someone approaches you with an investment opportunity that sounds too good to be true, run. The only investments where there aren't any risks are CDs, money markets, and government-backed savings bonds. All other investments require some level of risk. That is why you must strategically and carefully establish and maintain positive relationships with people you trust and believe in.

Unfortunately, money changes people's behavior. When someone comes into a large sum of money for the first time, they sometimes change for the worse. You want to be opposite of the this type of individual. Don't let money change you for the worse. Instead, let it mold you into a better person. You want to help and give to those who are less fortunate. Possibly help create jobs by starting or growing a business. Fundamentally, it all goes back to those professionals you have and are communicating with regularly regarding your finances.

Here are some strategies to establish and maintain positive relationships.

- Seek counsel on the right person that will help you achieve your financial goal.
- Do your homework about a particular professional and the subjects you will be seeking assistance with. You don't have to be an expert. Just by knowing a little about the subject and the professional will guide you to ask the right questions. Based on the professional's response, you will have a sense of whether they are telling you the truth or not.
- Get references. Seek out those referred to you by family, friends, clergy, and others whose opinion you value and trust.
- Keep an open mind. Don't have a know-it-all attitude.
- Perform due diligence. Read reviews, if available, about the person's past performance and the results achieved.
- Use Godly wisdom in all you do. Don't take someone's word without verifying the facts.
- Listen more than you talk. Sometimes we learn more by listening and by not saying a word.

- Be attentive. Know what's going on around you. Don't put your head in the sand and say you are not going to be a part. Stay relevant.

Chapter Questions

- *Do you have an open mind?* If the answer is no, consider modifying that stance to transition to someone who will at least listen to others. You may be surprised at how much you don't know and how much there is yet to learn from others.
- *Are you current with what's going around you and in our world today?* If the answer is no, I suggest you get involved immediately to stay relevant. With the advent of technology, change is occurring so rapidly most of us can't keep up.
- *Are you an introvert or extrovert?* If you are an introvert, try to step out of your comfort zone to meet people and begin to establish positive relationships. The only way to meet someone like yourself with similar interests is to step out and do something that you haven't done before. If you are an extrovert, continue to expand your quest of meeting and greeting different individuals. Weed out the ones who are not positive.
- *Do you have a discerning spirit/gift?* If the answer is no, ask God to give you one so that you may be able to assess whether a relationship will be good or bad for you.
- • *Are you a good listener?* If the answer is no, try to become one. There is so much that we can learn from others, if we only stop talking, sit, and listen.
- *Do you value what your family, friends, and co-workers say about others?* If the answer is no, consider how much your family loves you and wants the best for you. They would not recommend or steer you wrong in any circumstance. Similarly, friends and co-workers have a reputation to uphold when they refer you to someone. They want to hear and expect to receive positive feedback on the recommendation they gave you.
- *Do you research a professional before seeking them out?* If the answer is no, start to conduct research and read reviews on the performance this professional has achieved. This

should be done before you select them as a partner in your quest to establish and maintain positive relationships.

CHAPTER 7

DON'T TAKE NO FOR AN ANSWER

Just because someone told you that a goal or action could not be accomplished does not mean have you to accept it. All things can come to pass with some elbow grease and grit, even a goal that seems insurmountable.

Someone else's opinion does not have to become your reality. Even if a friend or relative tells you there is no way you can become president of the United States, quickly dismiss their comment, and do not accept it. The only thing stopping you is you. You determine what goals are set for you. You determine when to take action. You determine what college or trade school to attend. You decide to start a business or not. You methodically create multiple streams of income.

The bottom line is don't take no for an answer. This is particularly true when problem-solving or trying to get to the bottom of an issue. And it seems everywhere you turn, someone or something is telling you no or refuses to give you the correct answer so that you can make a rational and logical decision.

Acceleration Tip #6–Insist on Succeeding

Not taking no for an answer is equally applicable to growing wealth and maintaining it. The first step is to use different strategies to grow wealth. This is possible but not without blood, sweat, and tears. Growing wealth is achievable, but you have to set a deliberate course and take risks along the way to achieve this major milestone.

Accept the challenge and acknowledge the difficulty, but do it anyway. Take the obligation as well as the responsibility that comes with it. When you are obligated, responsible, and determined, anything can be done.

No is not an option. The plan is in place toward where you want to go. Yes, you can set financial milestones and complete each one. You can become a millionaire if, and when, you apply the concepts of living debt-free, investing in your company's 401k, developing multiple streams of income, using coupons, and asking for discounts at various merchant's place of business, making your money work for you, and living life on your terms.

People are constantly overcoming adversity, whether it's being an immigrant, coming from dysfunctional families, being orphaned, growing up in poverty. They did not use their circumstances to prevent them from achieving their financial goals. And neither should you. They said: *No words or statements will dictate to me what I will become. Yes, I am making this determination. It both starts and ends with me.*

These individuals are called winners. God made all of us winners. We just have to decide if we want to be a winner or a loser. Life and death is before us; the decision is up to us. This is particularly important when someone is pondering whether they can become a millionaire amid rising interest rates, the colossal US national debt, manufacturing jobs moving overseas, and other negative economic news. The answer is yes, you can still become a millionaire or whatever you desire to by simply telling all these negative indicators: *No, I am not obligated to yield to the negativism in the atmosphere. My number one responsibility is to believe that I can achieve the ultimate.*

Chapter Questions

- ***Have you been told that you cannot achieve a certain goal/ objective?*** If the answer is yes, shrug it off. I'm not saying don't heed to wisdom if something you are about to do may harm you or someone else mentally, financially, or even physically. But if it is just a plain declarative that you are not capable of reaching a feat, ignore it and continue in that direction, knowing you can and will defy the odds.
- ***Do you believe (sincerely) that you can accomplish anything you set your heart and mind to do?*** If the answer is no, then

read Philippians 4:13 in the Bible, and commit it to memory. Remember that scripture states unequivocally that you can "do all things through Jesus Christ who strengthens you".

- ***Do you embrace the title of this chapter?*** If you answered yes, then you are more than half way there. Thinking is believing. This can be positive or negative. Remember the adage that if you think you can't, you are right. Similarly, if you think you can, you are also right. That's why you must not take no for an answer. Only God can tell us no. No other person has the authority or latitude to dissuade us.
- ***Do you now accept the real concept that you can become a millionaire/billionaire?*** If the answer is no, review what has been covered in this book thus far, starting with accepting Jesus Christ as your personal savior to refusing to take no for an answer.
- ***Have you encountered adversity in your life?*** If the answer is yes, this represents reality for everyone. If the answer is no, it will show up sooner or later. The objective here is to encourage you to press through the adversity that you have or will go through. Tell the adversity: *No, I am not going to submit to you. Instead, I am going to meet you head on and overcome whatever is facing me or holding me back from my aspirations.*
- ***What set of circumstances makes you accept a no rather than a yes?*** Here's an opportunity to spell out what holds you back from doing what you know you need to do. Is it a family member? Money? Drugs? Lack of employment? Mindset? Lack of confidence? No motivation? Lack of education? One of the solutions to overcoming our inhibitions and fears is to speak the word of God about our lives and problems. When we do this, we can easily say yes rather than no.

CHAPTER 8

CARPE DIEM

Carpe diem is usually translated from Latin as *seize the day*, taken from *Odes* by the ancient Roman lyric poet Horace. I'm using it here to remind you that opportunities, youth, vitality, and motivation don't always exist. Therefore, those of us who have a unique chance must seize the day. If not, that special moment in time will be lost and gone forever.

We get to be 18 years old only once in life. The world is our oyster because nothing can stop us. Simply put, this means that nothing or no one can preclude us from achieving our purpose in life. We are smart, intelligent, healthy, and whole in our bodies and our minds. But many of us pass up critical chances to go all the way and live to regret it. Can you visualize being 18 years old again? Oh, how you would do things differently. That is guaranteed. You and I both would have a do-over in our lives.

I use carpe diem because I want to emphasize that you must be at the right place at the right time doing the right thing to take advantage of everything given to you. When the stars align, you can accomplish the improbable, including shaping your financial future. It also means putting into practice living a debt-free life, charting a course for your life, and ensuring you get paid for what you're worth.

Carpe diem reminds us to take charge of the day and run with it. Whether it's focused on finances, health, or relationships, it doesn't matter. What matters most is that those once-in-a-lifetime chances are exploited and maximized to your benefit and possibly others', which no stone is left unturned, and nothing is left on the table. This is the type of mentality you want to employ when pursuing your financial destiny.

An example of capitalizing on carpe diem is to begin using dollar cost averaging when the stock market has decreased in value. This approach simply states that shares of individual stocks are currently lower in value than they previously were. The way dollar cost averaging works is to purchase a finite number of shares each week or month, regardless of the rise and fall of the individual stock price. The end goal is to accumulate more shares over time and grow your portfolio. How will growth occur? The growth will occur in buying the stock at different prices over an extended period, which will lend itself to amassing shares that are now at a higher value.

What I am emphasizing is you have to take the necessary steps when the opportunity presents itself and invest in the market. Or invest in yourself by getting training or certification in a sought after technical skill. There are numerous federal and private jobs available for those ready to begin work. And they will get paid what they are worth. It's all a matter of timing. Get trained. Get noticed. Get hired. Get paid.

Here are other examples of seizing the day when it comes to investing. Look at some of the companies we patronize to buy cell phones, use search engines, and share pictures. All these multinationals launched Initial Public Offerings (IPOs). As the name implies, an IPO is when a new company sells shares to the public. When they first launched their IPOs, their stock prices were low. Currently, most of these same companies have a three-digit value per stock. Those investors who seized the moment and purchased them at the IPO offering and kept accumulating are extremely wealthy today. Once again, we see the connection between taking advantage of unique opportunities, taking action, and using timing to expand and grow for the future.

Carpe diem is not only useful in striving for great financial aspirations. It is equally applied to relationships, acts of kindness, volunteering, visiting prisoners in prison, feeding the homeless in shelters, and other worthwhile feats that should be done. It does not discriminate. Anyone can take use of the day and make it count for something. A kind word is often more valuable than money or gold.

Can you believe a stranger took a chance and made someone else's day by reaching out to them in a special way? The stranger may have provided food, clothing, or protection from the elements to those who are in need. There are different ways we can make good use of the time that we have on earth. Whether it is through good deeds or sharing love with others, it doesn't matter. What is important is that we do something to help ourselves as well as others.

Here are ways to breathe life into carpe diem.

- Before you can seize the day, you must have a vision for your life. You must believe that you are going to improve your lot.
- Don't forget to dream of achieving something that's good and great.
- People and circumstances are placed in our paths for a reason.
- Recognize when a special opportunity is before you. Do not ignore it. Accept it as fate. It was meant for you.
- You are young only once. Use it to your advantage. When we are young, we can do so much more. Our thinking is clearer. We have fewer responsibilities. We have strength. Capitalize on your youth and all its energy.
- Try something (honest and forthright) that you have never done before.
- Use time as an ally. The best example of this is when you are planning and investing for the future. The sooner one begins to invest, the sooner the financial goal will be achieved.

Chapter Questions

- ***Have you seized every opportunity put before you?*** If the answer is no, what was missed is history. You can begin this day by not passing up on special opportunities that were specifically for you. This once-in-a-lifetime treat may have been a job, a promotion, an investment, a true love, a chance to share love with someone who felt unloved, a unique experience to visit those in prison, or to feed the homeless.
- ***Do you believe you have what it takes to achieve something that's good and great?*** If the answer is no, get a larger vision of yourself. There is something special in each one of us. It may be singing, acting, preaching, serving, litigating, giving, parenting, volunteering, or planting. We simply have to find out what it is God has placed inside us.
- ***Were you ever afraid to try something that you never did before?*** If the answer is yes, now maybe the best time to step

out and see what happens. This new venture may prove to be what you have been looking for.

- ***Are you afraid to seize the day?*** If the answer is yes, you must ask yourself why. Are you afraid that you might succeed? Are you concerned about what others might say about you? You need to answer these questions to fully implement this concept.
- ***Have you already tried to implement carpe diem in your life and it did not work?*** If the answer is yes, please explain why it did not work. What was the problem and what specifically precluded you from reaching your goal? When you review what prevented you from attaining the results desired, address that problem, person, or obstacle head-on. In other words, approach it from a different perspective. If an individual won't help you, then try someone else. If the free funds for an educational program are no longer available, apply to a different program that has free funds. If your business failed, try a different business after you've done your due diligence and researched the new venture. The bottom line is don't give in too soon. Continue to seek out what it is you are supposed to do on earth. Truly seize the moment, the day, the year, and even the life.

CHAPTER 9

SELF-ACTUALIZE

Everything we desire to do that is positive and beneficial for society as well as ourselves starts and ends with God. He gives us the authority and the know-how to accomplish any feat that we can conceive. However, He is a perfect gentleman and will not force His will upon anyone. In fact, He allows us to make the call about our lives and how we live them. This is because when we read His word, it directs us how to live and how to apply godly wisdom. In my opinion, all of us should use Godly wisdom in everything we do or attempt to do.

There are human hurdles we are supposed to negotiate as infants, toddlers, adolescents, pre-teens, teenagers, young adults, middle-age adults, and seniors. Yet on each step of this continuum, God will not interfere. He leaves it to us to fill in the details and get whatever we are supposed to get in overcoming those hurdles. God will not do it for you. But He will put in your pathway and within your fingertips everything and everyone you need to be successful. Then it's up to you to put the pieces together. This perspective is even present in sports and other group activities. The coach gives the strategy and motivates the team, but the players are ultimately responsible for achieving victory. So is it with allowing your greatness to come out and to be shared with the world.

What comes to mind is Abraham Maslow's hierarchy of needs. Maslow tried to display that only once our lower needs are satisfied—food, shelter, belonging, and safety—can we become all God created us to be. Simply put, once the routine tasks are out of the way, then it's time to rise to the occasion and excel at who you are. I am asking you to extinguish anything that stands in your way of fulfilling all God wants you to become. If it's your attitude, get it out of the way. Cross it off. Even a broken relationship. Cross that off, too. If someone is standing in your way and will not let you go to the next level, find a way to go around them to move past this roadblock.

You must find a way to break out and self-actualize, which is allowing everything that's in you to be manifested out of you. This ranges from creativity to special gifts to unique talents to the impossible. It's only so because you were created to do something special. God gave each of us something unique to share with the world. Self-actualization is the secret inside of us waiting to be discovered. It simply means that there is something in you that needs to find its way out of you and into the atmosphere. Once it is, the world will be changed forever. Look at examples where individuals discovered cures for deadly diseases or created inventions that changed the world forever. These achievements were developed or created by individuals who self-actualized in their respective area. We all have something special in us. But we have to give ourselves permission to upset the status quo by becoming what and who we know we are supposed to be.

Have you ever been at an event where a person might be singing, dancing, preaching, or speaking? It just so happens that you may possess one of those gifts. You said to yourself: *I can sing just as well if not better than the person that is singing right now.* The difference here is the person that is singing stepped out, but you haven't. They are doing what you have been called to do. That is your inner man telling you that it is time to unleash your concealed talent.

No, it will not be easy. No one will tell you when it's time. You must ask God to lead and guide you. There are so many stories waiting to be told about you. Yes, you! Because you have something special that we are all waiting to experience. We are waiting to use your invention in our everyday lives. We are waiting for you to arrive on the scene with your stuff. Look at the number of athletes and entertainers who become famous worldwide because they could let go of any inhibitions and go for it.

I want to encourage you to let go of anything that may be holding you back. Don't concern yourself with what others might think or say. Do what you desire to do and do it extremely well. This is true even if you have already achieved some level of greatness. You are still here on planet Earth, and that means there is more to do. Apply this attitude to growing your finances, and nothing will be able to prevent you from reaching the highest heights and deepest depths of financial independence.

The reason most of us don't soar to the level of being financially independent is that we subconsciously choose not to self-actualize because we are afraid of what we might become or achieve. Push fear out of the way. Open the gate and go for your dreams. Self-actualize and become all God wants you to become.

Here's how to self-actualize:

- First things first, ask God to show you what it is He wants you to do with your life.
- Once you find out what it is you are supposed to do, excel at it. Be your best at it all the time.
- Act on this gift and let it run its course.
- Don't let anyone deter you from releasing what is inside of you. Your gift could be the next revolutionary invention. It could be a cure for AIDS. Or cancer. Or dementia.
- Refuse to accept defeat. Defeat will try to show up. Ignore it and continue on the path that has been laid out for you.
- Accelerate with this gift and don't let up until you have become everything you are supposed to.

Chapter Questions

- ***Are you afraid to succeed?*** If you answered yes, change the way you think. Everything starts in our minds and goes to our hearts. If you are afraid to be on the national stage or to be singled out for doing something out the ordinary, ask God to give you the confidence whereby this fear will be eliminated. And you will be able to move up to the highest level possible in your thinking and doing.
- ***Are you afraid of what others might think about your higher level of achievement?*** If the answer is yes, don't focus on other people. Instead, focus on what you were born for and let it come to pass.
- ***Why haven't you taken the opportunity to self-actualize?*** If your answer is that you're either not sure or uncertain on how to go about it, follow the steps presented earlier on how to self-actualize. Don't skip any steps. Implement them and watch things happen that you would have never dreamed of.

- ***Have you tried to rise above it all only to be defeated in the undertaking?*** If the answer is yes, this is normal. We all will experience some degree of failure and disappointment. Get up, dust yourself off, and get back into the game of life. The more you try, the more likely you are to overcome an obstacle. Conversely, the fewer times you try, the more likely you will give up and stop trying.
- ***Do you believe you have already self-actualized?*** If the answer is yes, write out specifically how and when you finally arrived at your ultimate destination. What were you doing? How did it feel? What act assured you that you were at the place where you were supposed to be? Elaborate on these answers and assess them to see if you are truly where you are supposed to be in life.
- ***Do you know the first step you are supposed to embark upon to initiate the self-actualization process?*** If the answer is no, remember the first step is to ask God what He wants you to do. From there, the sky is the limit.

CHAPTER 10

DON'T FORGET TO REACH BACK AND HELP OTHERS

Now that you have attained financial independence, charted a course for your life, established and maintained positive relationships, become debt-free, and self-actualized, you must reach back to see whose hands are outstretched. Reach for them. In fact, extend your hand until it touches theirs, and then pull the other person up to where you are. We are stronger together. The more individuals that find the key to unlocking their world, the better we are as a community, as a country, as a nation, and a world.

Most of us haven't done what we can do because we didn't know what capabilities existed. However, when you come into the understanding of who you are and what you can become, then you can act and step out of the shadows into the light. Nothing is more rewarding than reaching back and helping someone who is trying to get where you are. Don't hoard newly acquired information. Instead, feel obligated to share the word to those who can benefit from your discoveries in life.

You learned how to get paid what you are worth. You did a self-assessment of your desired vocation accompanied by the appropriate due diligence to take the necessary time to research and read about the profession of your choice and its rewards. After the research and due diligence were completed, you stepped out on faith. From that point on, employers began to seek you out and offer tremendous compensation packages that you thought never were possible. You learned how to take the time and chart a course for your life. Later, you mapped out a game plan on how to get from the ghetto to Wall Street. Or how to get from being homeless to working at one of the tech giants in Silicon Valley. Or how to go from being underemployed to being employed just right.

Reaching back is a powerful tool to use in everyday life. It's contagious. It's effective. It's something that should be done 24 hours a day, seven days a week.

Chapter Questions

- ***Do you believe in reaching back and helping others?*** If the answer is no, put yourself in the position of not having essential information needed to move forward in life. A more eloquent way of presenting this is the problem of not knowing what you don't know. But when you hear it, you know it's just what you needed to advance in life. Furthermore, how would you feel if someone was holding information back from you? Probably not too kindly or neighborly. So it should be the same perspective you have about withholding knowledge from others. Once you share it, you will feel like you have saved a million people. When given a chance, help them!
- ***Has anyone ever reached back and helped you?*** If you answered yes, explain how it felt and what your reaction was when they did. If it was no, why do you think nobody has? Remember, this response is for you and you alone. I have many stories where supervisors, neighbors, friends, and even clients have reached back and shared with me some invaluable information. The first time this occurred was approximately 16 years ago. There was a hail storm that came through our county. After the storm had passed, I did not think any more about it. However, one of my neighbors told me his insurance company was paying for his new roof that was damaged during the storm. The neighbor recommended I contact my insurance company to see if I was eligible for a new roof as well. The answer I received was yes. You know the rest of the story. I was blessed with a new roof.

  This same thing happened about seven or eight years ago in a different house. Both roofs costs were in the five-digit category. Can you imagine if I had to pay out of pocket to replace those roofs? The point is, because my neighbor and the roofing company shared with me how I was eligible for a new roof, I saved thousands of dollars. Not to mention I received a new roof that will last from 15 to 20 years. Continue to reach back!

- ***Is there anything that would preclude you from sharing knowledge with others?*** If the answer is yes, what single thing is keeping you from helping others? Address it head on to ascertain if your view can be changed. Don't forget to put yourself on the end of not receiving valuable knowledge, delaying you from fulfilling your destiny for years to come.

SUMMARY

I hope you will buy into what was shared in this book. It was designed specifically for where you are in life. I made no assumptions about you or your aspirations. I was driven by a heartfelt sincerity to share with you what I have learned through the school of hard knocks. It's amazing how we can live all these years on earth and still not have the secret ingredients to success even though it is all around us. The Joneses have it. The Smiths, too! Even the Williamses. But somehow you've been left out. Well, not anymore. You now have the knowledge to conquer whatever goals you have set for yourself. You also have the wherewithal to realize when you have met the goals you set out for yourself and when it's time to set new goals and dreams. Remember, you are the one holding you back from accelerating your life financially and living life on your terms.

Accelerate!

GLOSSARY OF FINANCIAL TERMS

Annuity: This is an investment plan offered by insurance companies to guarantee a lifetime of income in retirement. There are fixed and variable annuities and many other hybrids.

Billionaire: Net worth is valued at least $1 billion.

Bonds: Private and public bonds; an example is a savings bond or bond used to build a school or a park.

Budget/financial plan: Your income vs. outgoing expenses.

Compounding interest: Interest that adds to the original principal and all subsequent years.

Debt-free: Nothing is owed. Completely free of debt.

Defined benefit: You receive a pension based on years of service and pay grade/position.

Defined contribution: You pay into your retirement account.

Direct investment program (DRP): when you can buy shares directly from a company.

Discount: Buy an item for less than its original price.

Dollar cost averaging: You invest a fixed amount weekly/ monthly/yearly regardless of the fluctuation in the daily price of the investment vehicle.

Initial public offering (IPO): A new company raises money (capital) through selling investors individual shares of stock.

Market value: What a willing buyer and a willing seller know about the facts at the time of purchase.

Millionaire: Net worth is valued at least $1 million.

Mutual fund: A group of individual companies combined into one investment. A hypothetical example is imagined if Walmart, Sears, Microsoft, Nextel, Gabe, and Apple are companies that make up one investment. This would serve as one-type of mutual fund.

Net worth: Your assets (home, car, furniture, stocks, bond, CDs etc.) less liabilities (mortgage, car loan, credit card debt) equals net worth. Example: $500,000 in assets less $300,000 in liabilities (what you owe) equals a net worth of $200,000.*OPM (other people's money)*: Someone else's money is used to purchase items.

Stock: When you own a share in a public company, such as Burger King, Giant Food Store, Walmart, Macy's, Payless, etc., you are a part of an individual company through your stock ownership.

Title insurance: Offers protection for the buyer when a background check is performed on the history of the property. It ensures there aren't any taxes in arrears, bank loans, personal loans, or other deed issues linked to the property.

Precious metals: Gold, silver, and the like.

Private mortgage insurance (PMI): Insurance mortgage lenders require you to have if you pay down less than 20% or refinance with less than 20% equity.

Real estate: Land and buildings.

Rental property/rental income: A parcel of real estate that is leased to another for a specific dollar amount over a specific period. Two parties are part of this agreement. The two are a lessor and a lessee. The lessor owns/manages the property, and the lessee pays the rent.

Rule of 72: A simplified way to determine how long an investment will take to double, given a fixed annual rate of interest. By dividing 72 by the annual rate of return, investors can get a rough estimate of how many years it will take for the initial investment to duplicate itself. An example is $100 invested at 8%. In this scenario, dividing 72 by .08 equals 9 years. So it will take nine years for $100 to double to $200.

SAMPLE MONTHLY BUDGET

Monthly Bills	Amount Due for the Month	Set Aside Column
Tithes	$ 425	
Offering	$ 40	
Medical Care	$ 48	
Dues	$ 10	
Grocery	$ 400	
Utilities	$ 150	
H20 & Sewer	$ 60	
Cell Phone	$ 110	
Telephone (Verizon)	$ 136	
Car Insurance	$ 250	
Life Insurance		$ 66
Emergency	$ 150	
AOL	$ 37	
Charity Donation	$ 325	
IRS	$ 200	
State Tax Payment	$ 100	
Subscription	$ 40	
Car Repair	$ 50	
IRA (Put on IRA check 2017 contribution)	$ 100	
Insurance	$ 100	
Mutual Fund	$ 250	
Savings Account	$ 400	

Vacation	$ 150	
Direct TV	$ 135	
ADT	$ 35	
Savings Bond	$ 125	
Credit Union Acct 1	$ 75	
Gas for Three Vehicles for 30 days		$ 300
Put Money in NFCU MEGI Savings	$1,000	
Main Gate Cleaners		$ 50
Sear's Washing Machine Maintenance Agreement		
Home Paramount		$ 60
Whirlpool Corporation		
Spouse Spending Money	$ 300	
Garage Door Opener	$ 50	
Christmas Club Account–put in short term	$ 100	
Parent's Birthday Gift		$ 50
Garbage		$ 40
Gift	$ 100	
Pay on Principal on Home Equity	$ 25	
Gas Heat		$ 50
Post Office	$ 10	
Dry Cleaning		$ 50
IRA, set aside	$ 250	
Pay on Mortgage Principal	$ 25	
Pest Control		$ 125
Savings for Family Members	$ 90	
Gift	$ 600	
Merrill Lynch	$ 250	
Buy Individual Stock	$ 300	
	$ 7,001	$ 791
Total Bills and Set Aside	$ 7,792	

Multiple Streams of Income:

Real Estate	$ 1,490
Pension 1	$ 754
Business Income	$ 1,800
Other Income	$ 10
Pension 2	$ 3,921
Total Income for November 2016	$ 7,975
Balance Remaining After Bills and Set Aside	$ 183

GRANTS

There are many sources of grants available from both public and private sources. For college, technical, and vocational training there are:

- Pell Grant
- Federal Supplemental Educational Opportunity Grants (FSEOG)
- Teacher Education Assistance for College Higher Education Grant
- Iraqi and Afghanistan Service Grants

The awarding of these grants is based on need and can also be merit based. Generally, you would have to complete the free application for federal student aid (FASFA) to qualify. In addition, each state and nonprofit offer a myriad of programs an individual may apply to and possibly qualify for.

There are grants available for first-time home owners to purchase a home. There are nonprofit grants for a variety of needs (education, medication, help with utilities, etc.)

Grants can be from private, federal, state, or nonprofit sources. To find out what government grants are available, go to grants.gov, which will tell you what grants are available, when the submission date is open, and when it will close. It will also tell how much can be awarded.

You'll need to identify other grants by researching on the Internet and then apply.

TIPS ON HOW TO CREATE INCOME THROUGH REAL ESTATE

Generating income through rental real estate is a part of the new mindset to create multiple streams of income. First, you need to determine if this is something that interests you. The average investor is not ready for rental real estate. It offers challenges, calls in the middle of the night, renters skipping out to avoid paying rent, declining property values and neighborhoods. However, if approached and managed correctly, it can help grow wealth over time.

I want to eliminate the idea of getting rich overnight. Each investment vehicle takes time to grow wealth. *Start early* and *stay the course* are words of wisdom when it comes to investing. Here are the steps for investing and buying rental real estate and avoiding the problems facing rental property owners.

- Identify in writing what resources you are going to use to buy these properties. Are you going to borrow from family and friends, use your savings, save up, cash in your 401k/403b, cash in your IRA, or acquire from other sources?
- Put in action your new-found knowledge of living debt-free. This includes buying investment properties cash.
- Research your local real estate market using the Internet to determine the price, the market, and the resale value of local properties. Here's a brief list of things to look out for.
    * Look into duplexes, triplexes, and fourplexes.

  * U.S. Treasury has seized properties for sale. Investigate these options.
  * Most major banks have properties they want to sell. See if any are available to you.
  * Inquire about someone you know is a motivated seller and wants to sell their property; the property may not even be listed, yet. This is the making of a potentially great deal.
  * Look for foreclosures everywhere.
  * Check with the county on unpaid real property taxes. Some states allow the payer of delinquent taxes (after a lapse of time, such as a two or three year waiting period) to apply for a deed to the property if the primary owner does not redeem his/her tax bill.
- Check out the neighborhood; don't buy in a war zone. Don't buy where you can't go and check on your property. Maintain your property in excellent condition. You will have long-term tenants.
- Decide if you are going to do flips rather than rent to others. You may opt not to rent but to buy a fixer-upper on the cheap, invest funds in it, and then sell it for market value.
- Don't be limited to where you live. Some areas such as San Francisco, Silicon Valley, Washington DC, New York City and other urban areas are too expensive to invest in rental real estate and make money. So you must look elsewhere for bargains. Consider taking on my perspective: I don't want a deal; I want a steal.
- Don't ever be too eager to purchase a property. This has happened to me, and I lived to regret it.
- Do your due diligence. Some properties have foundational problems, leaking roofs, cracked structures—the list is endless—that are cosmetically concealed. Always consider getting a licensed property inspector to check out the property from top to bottom before proceeding with the purchase. It's worth the investment of a few hundred dollars rather than spending tens of thousands after buying a property riddled with problems.
- Decide if you want to purchase single family homes or multi-family homes. The stability of the tenants is

important if you decide to rent. Some experts believe that single family home tenants rent for longer periods. However, when the property is vacant, no income is coming in. Conversely, a multi-family property generates income even when one unit is vacant. This step requires research and investigative work to determine which type of property you prefer and the availability of those properties. In short, this is your homework assignment.

- After you have completed all nine of the previous steps and you have narrowed down the potential properties, you can hire a real estate agent to write up a contract. Or you can do it yourself and save thousands of dollars. Agents typically charge anywhere from 3% to 6% of the sales price of the property. But this varies by state and jurisdiction.
- Don't make buying property complicated. All you need is a willing and qualified buyer and a willing seller. The rest is simple. Ask the seller what is the least amount they will accept for the property. Negotiate. Negotiate. Negotiate. There is always room to negotiate with the seller if they are motivated to make a deal. Both buyer and seller should agree to a reasonable price for the property. If the contract was written up by you, hire a local title company to do your closing. The title company is responsible for getting title insurance on the property, (which protects you in case there are liens present), recording the deed, paying any delinquent taxes, and ensuring all facets of the property are transferred from the seller's name to yours. The cost of the closing cost can be $600 and up. Both seller and buyer share in paying the closing costs.
- Don't transfer any money until you are satisfied there aren't any liens on the property. The property must be free and clear. Make sure you are completely satisfied with the final walkthrough. Everything you agreed to with the seller must be finalized before you pass the money. Typically, there are minor repairs that need fixing, and the seller agrees to take care of these before closing. I have been burned on these, too. Please learn from my mistakes.

- Because you are buying with cash, you have leverage in that you have the money. You have to be reasonable, but what you want and say carries a lot of weight in the transaction. Only buy houses that are in the best of condition. The roof, the furnace, the hot water heater, the water lines, foundation, structure and other major components should be in excellent condition if not new.
- The deal is done. Decide if you are going to manage the property or hire a local property manager, who will generally charge 10% of the rent collected. If you don't want the day-to-day hassle of managing the property, from collecting rents to responding to leaking toilet calls, consider a property manager.
- Here's a deal that was completed in October 2016. The location of the property is a lower middle-class neighborhood in New York. The purchase price was $29,000 cash. No real estate agent was involved, so there weren't any real estate commissions. The seller wrote the sales contract and the buyer accepted. An attorney conducted the closing. The property is an older home built in 1900. But it has a new roof, new furnace, new water line, and new hot-water heater. It has four bedrooms and one bath. The monthly rent is $700. The monthly expenses are as follows:
  - property manager, $70
  - fire insurance, $24
  - waste management, $14.25
  - water and sewer, $25
  - property taxes, $25
  - repairs set aside, $25
  - tenant fee, .83

  Net rental income estimated, $515.00
- Finally, let's look at your return on investment (ROI). You paid $29,000 for the property. The estimated net rental income is $515 per month or $6,180 a year. Dividing $6,180 (net rental income) by $29,000 (purchase price/initial investment) equals a return on investment of 21%. Keep in mind this is a best-case scenario. There will be repairs, thereby reducing your return on investment percentage.

These tips apply to first time home buyers as well as the more experienced real estate investor. Managing money does not discriminate. If you manage your resources wisely, these strategies will work for you as well. If you don't manage resources wisely, the strategies will not work for you. Money does not remain in the same location very long if it's not managed correctly. You may have to start with the least expensive property. But it still works and can grow your wealth over time. It is all matter of what you want to do.

Summary

Each transaction is different based on the condition of the house, the location of the house, the purchase price, where the property is rented, and the ROI. Proceed cautiously and carefully in the pursuit of buying, renting, and possibly selling rental real estate.

TIPS ON HOW TO GET STARTED WHEN YOU DON'T KNOW WHAT TO DO

When you don't know what to do, start from right where you are. This means beginning to lean in towards where you want to go. Write out those goals on where you want to go for the future. Then create a budget and follow it. Defined goals that direct your behavior in the direction you desire to go. This is key in everything we aspire to do. Secondly, the budget will quantify your dreams in terms of what income you have coming in and what you have going out. If you are in control of your finances, you have the challenge of growing financially independent halfway defeated.

Once you have established goals and adhere to a budget that you follow, you are progressing in the area you want to excel in.

After defining what your goals are and gaining control of your money, then slowly integrate the guidance from the ten chapters of this book into your strategy of moving forward in life. Afterwards, watch your financial life begin to take form and grow. You still have to manage it. But now it is on track.

TIPS ON HOW TO REDUCE MORTGAGE INTEREST

These tips are to help you save or reduce the amount of interest you would have to pay for your mortgage. If refinancing is something you desire, here's a plan to do just that.

Step 1: Review the terms, conditions, and length of your current loan. Specifically, look to see if there are any pre-payment penalties or clauses that prevent you from paying the mortgage off early. Also look to see if you are paying private mortgage insurance (PMI). PMI is insurance require when your down payment is less than 20% of the purchase price of the home. Once the loan reaches 80% of the home's original value, the lender is supposed to remove the PMI from the loan and reduce the mortgage payment accordingly. If not, contact the lender and request them to remove PMI from your loan.

Step 2: Calculate the cost. The cost of refinancing is typically 3 to 6 percent of the loan. The closing costs can be included in the loan, so you won't have to pay that out of pocket. But the closing costs will increase the amount of the new loan. There must be a cost benefit analysis done at the outset to ensure it's feasible to refinance.

Step3a: Consider refinancing if it makes economic sense. The point here is to make sure the rate you desire to refinance is as least 2% less than what you currently have. Otherwise, the cost may outweigh the benefits, at least in the short run.

Step 3b: Once you decide to refinance, consider taking out a shorter loan such as a 15-year loan, which will significantly reduce the amount of interest you'd pay over the life of a longer loan.

If you desire to keep your existing loan but still want to payoff it early, you can request to take your existing monthly mortgage and make two separate payments every two weeks, as discussed earlier in the book. Check with your lender to see if there is a fee to set up making biweekly payments. If there is a fee, ask if this could be waived.

You can also make extra principal payments. Request a copy of the amortization schedule from your lender to review the number of payments remaining. You should be able to see each month how much is due and how much is going to the principal and interest. Your emphasis is on the principal. That is, you want to pay down the principal as quickly as possible. The principal is paid down by making extra payments on the principal each month or as frequently as possible.

When you pay your monthly mortgage, add an additional amount and specify that you want this extra going to the principal. There isn't a specific dollar value that should be paid. It could be $25, $50, $100 or even $1,000. Cutting back on dinners out or going to the movies would allow you to apply those funds to the principal amount.

Some experts caution about paying off your mortgage early because of tax implications. I challenge that view. If you pay off your mortgage early and you are still working, that money goes into your pocket. I call it the eighth wonder of the world. You are still responsible for the taxes and insurance for the property. However, the dollar amount that previously went to the principal and interest now belongs to you. It is true that you lose the tax deduction for the interest. Who would you rather have the principal and interest for twelve months, you or the bank? I believe the answer is you. This debt-free mentality will require some tax planning.

Whether it is refinancing from a 30-year to a 15-year mortgage; commencing a biweekly payment using the same dollar amount for the existing mortgage payment; getting rid of PMI; or making extra principal payments, these strategies work if implemented.

TIPS ON HOW TO START CONTRIBUTING TO YOUR 401K/403B AT WORK

Usually, you would contact the human resources (HR) or payroll office at work that you desire to start or increase your contribution to the company's retirement plan/program. Keep in mind that you will have to adjust your budget because you will have less take-home money each week or month. However, this will help you begin the process of creating wealth, paying less in taxes, and deferring your federal income and state taxes. The more you contribute to your retirement the less you pay in taxes.

Also, don't forget to ask HR what's the company's 401K/403b investing in. Inquire about the actual investments. Are these investments stocks, bonds, mutual funds, high risk, low risk, or moderate risk?

Make sure to ask about historical performance. Albeit historical performance isn't a prediction for the future, it does give you an idea of how the investment vehicle has performed.

When choosing an investment to place your retirement in, always generate lots of questions. The more questions you have, the more informed you will be.

TIPS ON HOW TO PURCHASE A CD OR MONEY MARKET FUND

You have a plethora of choices here. You can shop around banks and credit unions to see which one offers the highest rate of return for the least amount invested. Do your homework. Don't be hasty. Compare at least five different institutions to see which ones give you the biggest bang for your buck.

Remember, certificates of deposit (CD) and money market funds come in different denominations. Some of these investments can be purchased for as little as $50. Challenge your financial institutions to answer the following questions:

- What is the minimum amount required to invest?
- How long is the term of investment?
- What interest rate is the institution paying?
- Are there any penalties associated with early withdrawal?
- Is my investment insured by the federal government?

TIPS ON HOW TO OPEN AND START CONTRIBUTING TO AN IRA (INDIVIDUAL RETIREMENT ACCOUNT)

Decide on which IRA you want to contribute to. There are different kinds of IRAs available on the market. The two most common are the traditional and the Roth, which is by far the most popular because you pay taxes on it when you initially invest the funds. Later, when the Roth IRA grows to a large amount no taxes are due at that time. For example, let's say you invest $1,000 today in a Roth IRA and it grows to $25,000 in 10 years. You then decide to withdraw the funds. Because you qualify to receive retirement under the IRS tax code (age 59 and a half under current tax laws), no taxes will be due on your $25,000 withdrawal.

You can purchase these IRA investments at banks, credit unions, investment professionals, and other finance and investment companies. Don't forget to employ the art of establishing and maintaining positive relationships.

Under current tax law, the annual limit that you can invest is $5,500 if you are under age 50. If you are over the age of 50, you may qualify to invest up to $6,500 in a single year. However, there are limits on IRA contributions based on your annual earned income.

Pose deep-seated questions (best rate of return, limits on contributions based on your annual earned income, withdrawal penalties if under age 59 and a half based on current tax laws, etc.) to whatever bank, credit union, or financial institution you decide to patronize in purchasing an IRA.

TIPS ON HOW TO ESTABLISH BIWEEKLY MORTGAGE PAYMENTS

The hidden secret of the biweekly payment option comes from the fact that there are 52 weeks in a year, thus you'd have 26 payments. If you were to simply make two payments a month that would be just 24 payments in a year, so actually the biweekly method has you making two extra payments each year, which is the same as making one extra monthly payment.

The mechanics of how it works is better when an example is given. Let's say your current monthly mortgage payment is $2,500. Over the course of a year, you will spend $ $30,000 on twelve payments. If you decided to make biweekly payments you can then make a $1,250 payment every two weeks. Doesn't it appear to be the same thing? No, not exactly. Well, if you take $1,250 and multiply it by 26 payments you have $32,500 in total payments. See what happens. That extra $$2,500 was applied directly to your principal, thus reducing how much you'll spend on interest and helping you pay your mortgage off faster.

To make it clearer from a savings perspective, consider a $250,000 30-year mortgage at 5%, you'll pay $233,139.46 in interest, plus the $250,000 principal, for a total of $483,139.46. Paying one-half of your regular monthly mortgage payment every two weeks will result in interest of $190,193.73, a savings of $42,945.73. Obviously, the larger your mortgage and higher your interest rate, the greater the savings.

So switching to a biweekly payment is as simple as splitting your monthly payment in half and making a payment every two weeks, right? Well, hold on just a minute. While that is the general idea, you do want to check with your lender first. For one, you might already have an established automatic payment and you'd want to make sure you could stop that. Otherwise, you might find yourself paying even more.

Also make sure that your lender will accept biweekly payments. While most lenders should, there are cases where they will not, or if they do, the extra money might not automatically be applied to the principal. You must have a lender that will immediately credit each half monthly payment upon receipt. If your lender waits until the second payment has been received before crediting your loan, you'll never see the benefits.

Be sure to check to see if your mortgage has a prepayment penalty. If you are in doubt about this being in your mortgage agreement, ask your lender. Typically, in the current environment in which we live, prepayment penalties are seen less often. However, you have to verify with 100% assurance that this clause is not a part of your loan agreement. Check it out for a peace of mind and accuracy. Then proceed accordingly.

Caution as You Proceed to Implement Biweekly Payments

Because adopting biweekly payments is a very useful tool in helping you pay less in mortgage interest, there are many scams that will promise you the world and deliver you nothing. So proceed cautiously as you attempt to change from a monthly payment to a biweekly payment. The best advice is to make this change with someone you trust. Many options exist to implement a biweekly mortgage payment. Some banks/finance companies may charge you a fee. Others do not. You shouldn't have to pay a fixed fee or $500 or $600 for this change. When you communicate with your mortgage company and they opt to charge a fee, decline the offer. A way around this hurdle is to make one extra payment each year. This strategy has the same effect as the biweekly option. The only difference in this scenario is that you are introducing additional money into the equation. Conversely, with the biweekly payment feature, no new money is being introduced into the strategy.

TIPS ON HOW TO PURCHASE AN ANNUITY

An annuity is an agreement with an insurance company to offer you a type of retirement income for life or a finite number of years. Where do you go to purchase an annuity? Because you have established positive relationships with investment professionals you trust, you can inquire of your banker, your investment professional, or your current insurance provider. As always, get all the facts. Annuities come in all flavors. So ensure you get the pertinent information you need to move forward, if this is a part of your investment strategy.

Annuities have been known to have high investment fees. Ask the financial institution what the fees are for their annuities. Also ask for an explanation of the types of annuities to find the one that's just right for you.

Annuities come with a guaranteed rate of return on your purchase. Ascertain what your guaranteed rate of interest will be.

What impact is there if you withdraw your contribution before you reach age 59 and a half?

Ask the representative to explain the difference between a variable and fixed annuity.

Have them explain the pros and cons of owning an annuity.

TIPS ON HOW TO PURCHASE MUTUAL FUNDS

Buying mutual funds is similar to buying other investments: you can buy them through your investment professional or your banker who has mutual funds as a part of their business portfolio. Schedule a one-on-one session with the financial institution you feel most comfortable with. See what they have to offer and then review your financial goals to ensure it fits into your overall financial plan. The good thing about mutual funds is you can start with a small amount. Inquire about whether the funds are load or no load. No load funds mean there isn't a fee to you the investor. Conversely, load means there is a fee charged to you as the investor. Ask what is the minimum amount required to invest. You may only have $50 per month to invest. See if you meet the minimum criteria to invest. Make the adviser do a thorough review with you and answer all your questions.

TIPS ON HOW TO PURCHASE INDIVIDUAL STOCKS

There are numerous ways to purchase individual stocks. First, look at which stocks you desire to invest in. A rule of thumb is to consider the hottest companies that are planning on launching an IPO. The second is to invest where you spend your money: cell phones, consumer goods, groceries, restaurants, technology companies, shipping companies, clothing manufacturers, coffee makers, oil companies, green energy companies, car companies, airline companies, do it yourself stores, and the list goes on. Invest with your conscience.

You can buy stocks yourself on a number of different websites. Computershare is one. TD Ameritrade is another. Or you can use an investment professional or your banker. Be mindful of the fees that are charged. Sites such as computershare, TD Ameritrade, and others charge a minimum fee. However, investment professionals and banks charge a higher fee. Therefore, you have to decide if you have the time to buy and sell individual stock. The concept remains the same: buy low and sell high.

Always use caution when you purchasing on the Internet. Use wisdom in all things.

TIPS ON HOW TO START AN EMERGENCY FUND

During your budget preparation and allocation of your income against your expenses, remember to incorporate an emergency fund line item into your weekly or monthly budget. You could set aside $10, $20, $30, $40 or more per week/month just for emergencies. These funds are not used for everyday expenditures. They should be labeled as an emergency and used as such.

Your emergency fund should be stashed in an account that's earning the highest rate of return without committing the funds to an extended period-of-time. Should an emergency arise, you should be able to access these funds immediately and put them where they are needed.

Explore what accounts are available to open for an emergency. Credit unions generally have the highest rate of return. But be sure this is the case. Do your due diligence and shop around.

TIPS ON HOW TO START A CHRISTMAS/BIRTHDAY/ VACATION OR OTHER FUND

Starting a Christmas, birthday, vacation, or other fund is a must to build and grow your nest egg. These kinds of expenditures can take a toll on your finances. You must plan for them each time you receive compensation or multiple streams of income. Set aside an amount for each category every month. So when these special days arrive, you will have saved an entire year for them. They will not derail your financial goal of accelerating and winning.

Identify what financial institution you desire to set aside these funds in so the money is safe, accessible, and earning a competitive rate of return.

TIPS ON WHEN TO PLAN AND PAY INCOME TAXES

When you are projecting a tax liability of $1,000 or greater in a single year, the IRS recommends you begin making estimated tax payments. To do this, go to IRS.gov and complete form 1040ES (estimated income tax payment) and make your estimated tax payments. Of course, before you make estimated payments, include all your income on a dummy tax return. Then include your projected deductions and/or expenses if you happen to have a business. When this dummy return is completed, you will have an estimate of what you will owe.

This is done for two reasons: unless you have saved up an entire year, you are going to have a hefty tax bill when tax time arrives, and the IRS requires you to do this. Secondly, it also makes good tax sense to conduct tax planning to ensure you have enough money set aside for taxes and you have somewhat of an idea of what your tax liability will be a year from now.

Tax planning should also be done for the state you live in unless your state does not have an income tax. In this case, this state tax tip would not apply to you.

TIPS ON HOW TO APPLY FOR FREE STUFF, INFORMATION, AND ASSISTANCE

1. The U.S. Government has a list of domestic assistance programs available to both individuals and organizations for a variety of purposes. A catalog of federal domestic assistance programs is available at cfda.gov for specific information and instructions.
2. If you need help with housing, utility bills, medical bills, and other necessities, go to USA.gov and apply for help.
3. If you think you may have unclaimed money the government owes you, then go to USA.gov and click on unclaimed money. You will have a choice to search by state or the federal government, including the internal revenue service. Try it! You never know. You may find some money owed to you.
4. Anything you want to know about America that is not classified, you can request it under the Freedom of Information Act (FOIA). Go to FOIA.com.
5. If you are contemplating starting a business and you want to sell to the U.S. Government, you can sign up for free. There isn't a need to hire a vendor to sign you up. Simply go to sam.gov and follow the instructions to sign for free. After the System for Award Management (SAM) has processed your application, you are an official government vendor for free. Go to sam.gov and sign up.
6. After completing step five above, you can go to Federal Business Opportunities and review all the contracts the government has available to the General Public. Anyone

can bid on them. Not just the large defense contractors. Go to fedbizopps.cos.com and view all the contract work the government is seeking to hire others to complete.

7. Once you make the commitment of going into business, you can receive free counseling from the Small Business Administration (SBA) and the local procurement technical assistance program (PTAP).
8. If you are in need of food or temporary shelter, you can contact local churches and charities where you reside. In most localities, there are shelters in place to render assistance for basic living necessities.

TIPS ON HOW TO SEARCH FOR MISSING MONEY THAT MAY BE DUE TO YOU

You may have money that is owed to you. One of the ways you can search for possible unclaimed money is to go to missingmoney.com. From there, you can review all the links to where money may be found in your name or a family member's name. There aren't any guarantees, but this is possible. It's free research and may require some time. But it is available for you to see what is out there.

TIPS ON HOW TO BUY UNITED SAVINGS BONDS

As of January 1, 2012, the U.S. Government stopped selling saving bonds over the counter or at banks or credit unions. You must now purchase them online. You have to decide what type of savings bonds you desire to purchase. Go to treasurydirect.gov to review the different types of bonds available and interest rates available at the time you review the data. Also remember these savings bonds are backed by the U.S. Government 100%.

The I savings bond pays more interest than the EE series. Do a comparison when you are online and make a decision that fits into your financial goals.

TIPS ON HOW TO SIGN UP FOR THE NEW MYRA ACCOUNT WITH THE U.S. GOVERNMENT

The myRA is introduced here because some individuals don't have any type of retirement program. The U.S. Government created this savings to help out in this manner.

Who manages it?

Answer: The Department of the Treasury

What does it invest in?

Answer: A new United States Treasury retirement savings bond in the form of a Roth IRA

Can I lose money?

Answer: No, you cannot lose money. It's backed by the federal government 100%.

Is there a cost involved or fees associated with opening a myRA account?

Answer: No.

The maximum amount you can contribute to this account is $15,000. Once you reach $15,000, the Roth account is then transferred to a private Roth account. You can also withdraw the principal balance without penalty. The penalty free withdrawal does not include interest earned. Any interest earned would have to meet the minimum five year held rule under current federal tax laws. The bottom line is the principal can be taken out at any time without penalty. But the interest earned must the pass the tax rules before any exclusion.

There is no minimum balance required in this account.

Go to myRA.gov for more information, including on how to sign up with the Department of the Treasury.

TIPS ON HOW TO LEARN MORE ABOUT INVESTING

There are many resources to learn more about investing. A good place to start is the website www.investor.gov, which is run by the U.S. Securities and Exchange Commission's Office of Investor Education and Advocacy. This unbiased government website is intended to help individuals invest wisely and avoid fraud.

TIPS ON HOW TO EXPLORE WHAT YOU WILL RECEIVE FROM YOUR SOCIAL SECURITY

Can you plan on receiving social security when you retire? How much will you get? Where can you find this information?

You can learn more about Social Security and the level of benefits you can expect to receive by visiting Social Security's Retirement Planner at http://www.socialsecurity.gov/planners/retire/ and starting a *my Social Security* account, which can give you a customized estimate of your future benefits at http://www.ssa.gov/myaccount/.

There are strategies that show you how to maximize social security as well. Typically, the answer is mostly a delay in receiving your social security benefit (money). However, there are instances if your health isn't the best you may opt to receive social security benefits (money) initially upon becoming eligible. The commencement of receiving social security benefits should also be factored into how much other money you will be receiving at the same time. Since there is an amount you cannot exceed in other funds (not social security benefits) without being penalized by the Social Security Administration, it is wise to be informed about this threshold and the consequences of exceeding it.

Go to ssa.gov and review the facts on how much you can earn while concurrently drawing social security.

Other strategies may include married couples who may be different ages, where one is social security eligible and other is not. All of these factors must be considered when contemplating receiving social security benefits.

This is a very complicated matter and requires detail research and explanation. Please go to ssa.gov and present your specific scenario to the Social Security Administration.

Use Investment Exercise to Project How Much You can Save

This is a practical exercise you should try. Go to investor.gov. This is a government website that informs you about investing. When you get to the website, click on additional resources. Once you see what is available on additional resources, click on the compound interest calculator. It is here where you can do different scenarios to determine how much you can save if you invest a finite dollar amount at a given rate for a fixed number of years. Here's an example I did. I indicated that my initial investment was $1,000. In addition, I noted that my monthly investment is $300. The number of years is 40. The interest rate is 6 percent. My results yield $567,428.79. Yes, this shows once again the power of compounding interest.

Explore other what if scenarios based on the amount invested initially, the monthly contribution amount, the interest rate, and the number of years.

This trial and error will show you unlimited savings and investing possibilities.

EXAMPLES OF ORDINARY PEOPLE WHO ACCOMPLISHED EXTRAORDINARY FINANCIAL GOALS

I would be remiss if I didn't share with you a brief list of financial accomplishments made by ordinary people who were able to accomplish extraordinary financial goals.

A single female is totally debt-free. She owns her home and car outright. She works for the US Government. Her net worth is greater than $1 million. She pays for items in cash, maxes out her thrift savings plan (401k/403b equivalent), maxes out her IRA ($6,500 per year when you are age 50 or older), and gives to charity.

A single male has a net worth of $1.6 million. He works for the US Government. He took advantage of the dollar cost averaging and compounding interest financial engines. He stays with his game plan—invest no matter what the stock market does.

A husband and wife paid off their mortgage in less than seven years. They applied large sums of money towards the principal until the principal balance was paid in full. This was $200,000.

A husband and wife saved more than $1million. They used all the financial engines (stocks, bonds, real estate, annuities, and mutual fund) to achieve this financial status.

A husband and wife have a net worth of $2.4 million. They are self-employed. They used a business and the other financial engines to increase their net worth.

This is not meant to impress you, but to impress upon you what you can achieve if you are serious about accelerating your life financially. Get onboard and go up in the stratosphere.

HELPFUL LINKS

amortization-schedule.info/calculator – allows you to calculate your monthly payment

bankaholic.com/finance – used only for comparison of the highest certificates of deposit (CD) rates

cfda.gov – provides a list of federal domestic assistance programs offered by the federal government

dividend-stocks/dow-30-dividend-stocks.php – review 30 of the largest corporations that makes up the Dow Jones 30

fbo.gov – used to review what government contracts are available to general public; it also is a list of what the government is buying

fms.treas.gov/faq/unclaimed.html – explore if the government or others owe you unclaimed property

foia.gov – used for getting information available on the United States

foreclosures.bankofamerica.com/view – properties you can purchase from Bank of America

grants.gov – grants available from the US Government

investor.gov – gives the basics about investing from the government's perspective

irs.gov/ – to complete estimated tax forms for the federal government

loopnet.com/Duplexes-Triplexes-Fourplexes-For-Sale/ – search for multifamily properties for sale in the United States

missingmoney.com – explores the possibility of missing money owed to you myRA.gov – discusses myRA retirement program in detail and allows you to sign online as well

sam.gov – used to apply to become a government vendor or sell your expertise to the U.S. Government

sba.gov/ – if you desire to start a business and doing business with the government and want free counseling and advice, this can be your source

socialsecurity.gov/planners/retire/ – gives pertinent information about social security and retirement

ssa.gov/myaccount/ – gives key information about your specific social security by having your own account

studentaid.ed.gov/sa/ (used only if applying to attend college or some other institution of higher learning)

treasury.gov/auctions/irs/ – if you desire to purchase real estate from the US Government

treasurydirect.gov – used to purchase savings bonds and explore other federal financial matters

USA.gov – used for requesting help with housing, utility bills, medical bills, etc

BIBLE REFERENCES FOR ADDITIONAL SUPPORT

Acts 8:20

Deut 8:18

Eccl 10:19

Gen 17:27

Gen 23:9

Gen 42: 25

Jeremiah 32: 9

Mal 3:8

Matthew 22:19

Matthew 25:14-30

Matthew 6:24

Philippians 4:13

I Timothy 6:10

I Timothy 6:7

FINANCIAL COMMITMENT TO YOURSELF

I am asking each reader who buys or reads this book to commit to achieving his/her financial goals. For each person this will take on a different answer, perspective, or meaning. That's okay. But when you do commit and sign up for a specific goal, it takes on a life of its own. In order to make this commitment real and genuine, I suggest you consider the steps below in your daily commitment to accelerate financially. I, write your name here, , will

1. Develop a financial plan within 30 days of reading this book.
2. Invest at least 1 percent of my monthly take home pay within 60 days of reading this book.
3. Increase my investment at least 1 percent per year until the maximum is attained.
4. Use discounts and coupons whenever the opportunity presents itself based on my affiliation (military, senior, health care provider, club membership, first responder, etc.)
5. Get up to speed on the rule of 72 (my money doubles based on the interest rate and number of years that equal 72) and use it in my daily wealth accumulation effort.
6. Use dollar cost averaging (when I invest the same amount each month no matter how the market performs) in my investment strategy; I can take baby steps with this strategy and still make great progress.
7. Read and become knowledgeable about how to grow wealth.

8. Start an emergency fund within 6 months of reading this book.
9. Start a Christmas fund within 30 days of reading this book.
10. Start a vacation fund within 90 days of reading this book.
11. Get at least three estimates before making a major purchases (house, car, appliance, etc.).
12. Go online and read about the dow jones 30 stocks and what they represent.
13. Compare savings and loan rates among credit unions and banks within 60 days of reading this book.
14. Go online and become familiar with all the investment engines and the corresponding pros and cons of each (stocks, bonds, certificate of deposit, annuity, individual stocks, rental property, mutual fund, and businesses) before investing 1 cent.
15. Embrace the concept that it takes time to growth wealth.
16. Develop multiple streams of income (certificates of deposit, money market fund, bonds, part-time job, etc.) within 12 months of finishing this book.
17. Practice forbearance (control) in my spending.
18. Curtail the use of credit cards unless paid off 100% each billing cycle.
19. Use credit cards that generate cash back based on routine purchases.
20. Get credit under control if this is a problem.
21. Use strategies to pay off my mortgage earlier.
22. Attempt to save up first and buy high dollar value items cash.
23. Strive to live debt free.
24. Consider getting retrained when I am ready in a discipline that pays me for what I am worth.
25. Explore the possibility of sharing an invention or creation with the world that God gives me.

26. Do whatever is necessary to get on and stay on the path of success and happiness.

_____________________________ date:

sign your name here

www.ingramcontent.com/pod-product-compliance
Lightning Source LLC
Chambersburg PA
CBHW071500200326
41519CB00019B/5808
* 9 7 8 0 6 9 2 8 6 7 1 9 8 *